"Louise has brilliantly uncovered and revealed the original 'Psychology Book.' You won't be able to put this book down. Her questions and solutions through life-examples gently allowed me to examine my motives and bring my hurts to Jesus for healing. Thank you, Louise, for helping me 'dig a little deeper,' because healing always leads to freedom and a greater relationship with the Master Physician, Jesus Christ." -- Vilet Weaver, Author and Marketing Specialist

★★★

"Louise Looney's humorous stories will surprise and delight you even as she opens your eyes to deep spiritual truths. Everything she teaches is grounded in scripture, as applicable today as when Jesus Himself taught. She is fun to read, yet incredibly wise. As you turn page after page, you will feel you have made a forever-friend." -- Joanne Hillman, Author, *Counterfeit Coin*

★★★

"Louise Looney engages a delightful "take a friend by the hand" approach to teaching in her wonderful book *Splashes of Living Water*. Using a story-teller's approach, she imparts wisdom, instruction and wit. Highly recommended!" -- Janice Hanna Thompson, author of the Weddings by Bella series

★★★

As I edited Louise Looney's manuscript *Splashes of Living Water*, her words blessed me. In each chapter she shared her heart and soul. I know readers will enjoy this book as much as I did. – Janetta Messmer, Author/editor

Also by the author:

Using Your Dollars with Cents
In His Hands
Hidden Treasures for Golden Years, Winner of coveted Selah award as the best book on Christian Living for 2011.

Splashes of Living Water

Louise L. Looney

Inspiring Voices®
A Service of **Guideposts**

ISBN: 978-1-4624-0355-4 (e)
ISBN: 978-1-4624-0354-7 (sc)

Library of Congress Control Number: 2012918338

Inspiring Voices books may be ordered through booksellers or by contacting:

Inspiring Voices
1663 Liberty Drive
Bloomington, IN 47403
www.inspiringvoices.com
1-(866) 697-5313

Because of the dynamic nature of the Internet, any web addresses or links contained in this book may have changed since publication and may no longer be valid. The views expressed in this work are solely those of the author and do not necessarily reflect the views of the publisher, and the publisher hereby disclaims any responsibility for them.

Any people depicted in stock imagery provided by Thinkstock are models, and such images are being used for illustrative purposes only.

Certain stock imagery © Thinkstock.

All Scripture quotations are taken from the Holy Bible. The scripture references are as follows:

The Message (MSG) copyright 1993. Used by permission of NAV Press Publishing Group.

The King James Version of the Bible (KJV).

The New Century Version (NCV) copyright 2005 Thomas Nelson, Inc. Used by Permission.

The Holy Bible, New International Version (NIV) copyright 1975, 1978, 1984. International Bible Society. Used by permission of Zondervan Bible Publishers.

Holy Bible, New Living Translation (NLT) copyright 1996 used by permission of Tyndale House Publishers, Inc., Wheaton, Illinois 60189. All rights reserved.

Contemporary English Version (CEV) copyright 1995 by the American Bible Society. All rights reserved.

The New Revised Standard Version Bible (NRSV) copyright 1989 by the Division of Christian Education of the National Council of Churches of Christ.

The Amplified Bible (AMP). The Amplified Bible Old Testament, copyright 1965, 1987, by the Zondervan Corporation. The Amplified Bible New Testament, copyright 1954, 1958, 1987 by The Lockman Foundation. Used by permission.
Illustrated by Paul A. Looney, M.D.
Printed in the United States of America

Inspiring Voices rev. date: 10/24/2012

DEDICATION

Splashes of Living Water is dedicated to Carey, my husband of thirty-five years, who went to be with the Lord two and a half decades ago. The seeds of his ideas lay dormant for years until the Holy Spirit nudged me to get them out, plant and water them. Now, his dream has ripened into spiritual fruit that offers health and healing for the multitudes.

THE THIRST FOR SOMETHING MORE CAN
ONLY BE SATISFIED WITH LIVING WATER.

TABLE OF CONTENTS

FOREWORD

Louise Looney is one of my critique partners, but I first had the pleasure of meeting her during my visits to Hidden Manna, her retreat center in New Waverly, Texas. Though the center could only be described as a tranquil respite resonating with the peace of God, Louise was then, and is now, a fireball of energy, wit, wisdom and joy.

Her latest work, *Splashes of Living Water,* reflects those characteristics. But more than that, her book reflects the Word of God as told by a daughter of the King. You will find what I call "zingers" on every page. Like splashes of cold water on a tired face, these zingers of wisdom wake up a weary soul, and snap us back to the reality of Christ in a fallen and deceptive world. Testimonies of His grace are woven throughout the book, true stories of those who lived past their mistakes, shortcomings, and heartbreaking experiences by trusting in and relying on God and His eternal, infallible Word.

I do not *hope* you will enjoy—I *know* you will enjoy this precious book. You will tell your family, friends and neighbors to read it as well. And if you loan it out, good luck with getting it back. This is a book you will want to treasure and refer back to often, a "keeper" to add to your personal library.

Linda Kozar
Author
Babes With A Beatitude—Devotionals for Smart, Savvy Women of Faith, 2009, Howard/Simon & Schuster

PREFACE

The core of ideas for this book came from dusty notes in my closet, left there years ago by my late husband, Dr. Carey Looney, a well-known Christian psychologist. He challenged Jesus' believers to fill their emotional and spiritual "reservoirs" with *Living Water*. He assured them that when their cups overflow, they'll fill the lives of others.

After several unsuccessful attempts to put flesh and muscle on this skeleton of a message, I pulled out Carey's notes once again and prayed for enough wisdom to breathe life into his dream. The Holy Spirit nudged me and whispered, "Use your own voice in the book, not his." Then the ideas began to flow.

The different themes of the book are saturated with heartwarming and humorous stories wrapped with insight on how to live the abundant life Jesus intended. God did not create us to live in isolation, nor to fill our basic needs alone. These needs can best be met when we reach out in loving concern to those around us.

Each chapter sparkles with examples everyone can relate to. This gives the manuscript universal appeal. Now, after completing the task, I ask the Lord to pull back the clouds a bit and let Carey look down from heaven to find that his vision has become a reality.

Thank you, Lord, for watering my creativity in order to bring Carey's goal to fruition. My prayer is one he would endorse. "Let the message of this book change the lives of God's children and usher them into His rich and fulfilling purpose." The goal of each chapter is to be a stepping stone toward the end of our journey where we anticipate hearing the Father's loving approval, "Welcome home, faithful child."

ACKNOWLEDGEMENTS

My thanks and gratitude are extended to Joanne Hillman, Linda Kozar and Samuel Lanford who critiqued my writing and helped me chisel off the rough edges and polish the manuscript. Janetta Messner, you were very helpful in editing the book. Thanks to Vilet Weaver, who strongly believes in this message and stands nearby to cheer me on. Thanks to my son, Paul Looney, for your cartoons. You drew them almost thirty years ago and think they are amateurish, but I think they are great. Thank you Bette Lanahan, who came time after time to help me with computer problems.

But most of all, I thank my Heavenly Father, who gave me the insight and ideas and then prodded me until I finished the assigned task. I offer this book as a praise offering to God and ask Him to give the increase.

Thank you, loyal encouragers. You loved me enough to sand and polish my work to the point I'm ready to let it go.

ABOUT THE AUTHOR

Louise L. Looney, B.S. M.A.

Louise is a Bible teacher, author, speaker, teacher and mentor. She's taught in elementary through college levels, in the prison system and in an underground Christian School in a Communist country.

Her desire to touch and change people's lives was fulfilled in directing a Christian Retreat Center, *Hidden Manna,* for fifteen years. She also served as the Director of Spiritual Affairs at a psychiatric hospital.

She currently lives in Conroe, Texas and each week she teaches two Bible classes and facilitates a women's group that deals with women's issues.

Louise won the 2011 coveted Selah award for her book, *Hidden Treasures for Golden Years.* The contest was open to publishers, editors, agents and authors. It was chosen as the best book in Christian Living.

Her web site is LouiseLLooney.com

SECTION I
IT'S BROKEN, FIX IT

1

WHAT HAPPENED?

Time marches on

The lament of an Old Dutch proverb still whistles truth, "Too soon I get old, too late I get smart." With the advent of instant everything, we may wake up one day to find we're "instant old." What a shock. Perhaps we should stop driving through fast food places and popping things in the microwave. Well, good grief! Just because we get our food prepared more quickly doesn't mean we have to be in such a hurry to get through life. If we cram too many things in too little time, it's bound to turn out to be a jumbled mess.

The term "fast talker" wasn't a phrase coined to describe modern technology. However, through networking, communication is launched through time and space in a split second. It creates havoc when we spit out snippy remarks without considering what we're saying or how it comes across to others.

There's a danger that life in the fast lane may cause us to act as lemmings rushing over a precipice. "You have given me only a short life; my lifetime is like nothing to you. Everyone's lifetime is only a breath" (Psalms 39:15 NCV).

Today we demand instant gratification. We trash many things

that aren't up-to-date or no longer suit our fancy. This mindset isn't limited to cars and gadgets, but sad to say, it also includes marriages and other close relationships that are tossed aside because of petty differences.

Consider those who like to control—better known as control-freaks. They insist others respond immediately and do what they're told. Seldom do they have many friends or relatives who stick around for long.

I had a friend that fit this description to a "T". Jan★ had one son. He was the only person she was close to in her life, and she wanted to take charge of almost everything he did. Even after he was grown, depending on how he responded to her demands, she'd write him in and out of her will. She knew they needed each other, but didn't know how to turn him loose to become the person God created him to be.

What's wrong when our mindset becomes so distorted we destroy the ones we're supposed to love?

We're taught to take care of those who're hurting. Wise King Solomon spoke to this issue: "Never walk away from someone who deserves help; your hand is God's hand for that person. Don't tell your neighbor, 'Maybe some other time' or 'Try me tomorrow' when the money's right there in your pocket" (Proverbs 3:27-29 MSG). Paying attention to other's needs and reaching out to them could possibly unlock the windows of heaven for God's blessings to flow.

Life is About Relationships

Wouldn't it be wonderful if scientists could invent a ray gun that could zap bad attitudes and blast selfishness? I'm sure the one who obtained a patent for the idea would be a shoo-in for the Nobel Peace Prize.

But it is our responsibility to cultivate good relations with those we associate with, for their benefit and ours. This takes time and most of us need help. The book of Proverbs stresses the importance of wisdom, which is essential if we're serious about learning how to get along with others. We could compare it to panning for gold. It's necessary for us to slow down enough to sift through the everyday flow of life to find nuggets that will embellish our time together.

It gives us a way to garnish the bond until it becomes a priceless treasure.

If we fail to recognize the need to clean up our acts, we'll likely get dirty looks from others.

Speaking of dirt, that reminds me of laundry day. Mom washed clothes outdoors in all kinds of weather, using a gasoline powered washing machine and a hand cranked wringer. On sunshiny days, clothes were hung on lines in the backyard to dry.

Today, with almost no effort, clothes are cleaned and ready to wear again. I'd like to think we had a quick way for God to teach us how to relate to others with clean attitudes and pure lives. But it takes time and energy to scrub out the stains of self-centeredness. However, if we're willing to put forth the effort, our lives can be hung out for the wind of the Holy Spirit to blow through. The pain and hurts we've heaped on others will begin to evaporate.

We Demand Good Craftsmanship

My niece and nephew, missionaries in a third world country, called for a plumber to come back for the third time to work on their toilet. They chuckled when the workman returned, threw his tools down and grumbled in disgust, "That's the trouble with you Americans. You expect *everything* to work." This couple was aghast when they started to close a window in their seventh story apartment and the whole window unit broke loose and crashed to the ground.

Still another time, they flew on a national airline. As their plane was landing, the seat across the aisle from them ripped loose and tumbled down the aisle—with a woman in it! For later flights, they booked on a different airline.

We expect equipment to operate smoothly, yet we don't always take the time or put forth the effort to cultivate harmony among those we associate with. When abrasive edges of others scrape against our rough edges, the conflict often leaves us raw and irritable. Wouldn't it be wonderful if our dealings with one another could be fixed so they always worked?

Progress?

In the last twenty years, more books have been written and scientific inventions patented than any time in history. But our quality of life hasn't improved that much. The media is chocked full of "yucky" influences on morals and attitudes. Even when this information is not immoral or crude, it often puts an emphasis on *me* instead of *we*. That, no doubt, is the reason some call this the "Me Generation."

"Practically everything that goes on in the world—wanting your own way, wanting everything for yourself, wanting to appear important—has nothing to do with the Father …The world in all its wanting, wanting, wanting is on the way out—but whoever does what God wants is set for eternity" (1 John 2:15-17 MSG).

Our generation enjoys many conveniences and we enjoy many luxuries as well as having access to incredible technology. Our computers, smart phones, iPads, and Google, with all their features, require little effort to instantly extract information that once took days or weeks to retrieve. How different it would be if we devoted half our ingenuity to discover how to make others feel loved and wanted.

Before computers, a friend of mine who'd been out of the workforce for a number of years began working as a secretary. I asked how she was doing and she replied, "I'm doing great. I've gotten to the point I can erase thirty words a minute!" Why can't someone devise a method that would erase slips of the tongue that easily?

Using Our Resources

When I first married, my twelve-year-old brother-in-law acted as if he were enamored with me. He leaned close and grinned, "If I had a thousand dollars, I'd buy me a horse with half of it and give you the rest." My husband, Carey, stood nearby listening to his brother's attempt to impress me. He challenged him. "Mickey, if you had a dollar, would you give her half of it?" The boy stammered and began to crawfish as he fingered the dollar bill in his pocket.

It's sad that many of us think in terms of a big *if*—IF things were different, we'd act better and give more to the Lord and others. But we're stopped short by the question, "What are we doing with what we have?"

We may consider our resources small, but they're *not* insignificant. When Moses stood before a burning bush and God gave him the assignment to lead His people out of Egypt, Moses made an excuse. He said he couldn't speak well. God challenged him. "What do you have in your hand?"

Every shepherd carried a simple staff similar to the one Moses held. God demonstrated how the staff could be used to perform miracles. Whatever we have to offer to the Father may seem small. However, Jehovah God seems to delight in using little things in incredible ways.

Some Have Good Hearts

How encouraging when we see examples among God's children that reflect a loving concern for others. At Christmas, a group of men from a local church decided to buy bicycles for children who lived in a poor neighborhood. When they delivered the bikes, the children jumped up and down, squealing with delight. One of the benefactors began removing the price tags and a small boy came up behind him and tugged at his sleeve. In a wee voice he begged, "Please sir, don't take the price tag off mine, I've never had anything new before."

Thank you, Lord! We not only see generous people reaching out to the poor, but it's also heartwarming to see major outreaches following natural disasters. Compassionate individuals representing different ages come from all walks of life. Perhaps these *are* signs of changing winds.

Our Father equipped us with everything we need to enjoy our lives together, regardless of handicaps, financial ability or racial backgrounds. When we depend on God and believe He is everything we need, we'll realize that if our lives need a tune-up, we can check with the Manufacturer.

Stay Upbeat

If we want others to be around us, we must choose to be upbeat and remain cheerful. I have a friend with health problems who's in constant pain. However, if you ask how she's feeling, she smiles and responds, "Physically, this old body's a wreck and in a heap of trouble. But emotionally, I count on doing well as long as the Good

Lord lets me stick around." She refuses to allow the pain in her body to control her attitude.

My heart is touched by the words of the gospel pop song by Gene MacLellan who encourages us. "Put your hand in the hand of the one who stilled the waters. Put your hand in the hand of the one that calmed the sea." Holding to Jesus leads us to meaningful relationships with God and others.

We bear one another's burdens when we follow Jesus' example. "God's Spirit is on me; He's chosen me to preach the Message of good news to the poor—sent me to announce pardon to prisoners and recovery of sight to the blind. To set the burdened and battered free, to announce, 'This is God's year to act!'" (Luke 4:18 MSG).

It's exciting when godly people demonstrate Jesus' loving care. Faces glow with compassion and joy because of Christ living within. People are motivated to follow godly examples. We pray we are a prime example of Christianity—not with a doctrine to defend, but a way in which to live. When our lives are not self-centered, we embrace those that need a helping hand.

Lord, take our talents, time and gifts and use them. Give us greater compassion to share our blessings with others.

SCRIPTURES TO CONSIDER

Psalms 39:5
Proverbs 3:27–29
1 John 2:15–17
Psalms 33:20
Luke 4:18

QUESTIONS FOR DISCUSSION

1. The main thing I want to accomplish in life is . . .

2. Something I can do *now* in working toward that goal is . . .

3. When I'm feeling discouraged, I have an opportunity to . . .

4. When I start thinking negative thoughts I can . . .

5. I can reach out to the needy by . . .

6. Something good I could do today is . . .

7. The person who has been the greatest example for me in life is . . .
   The thing I most admire about them is . . .

2

BRING YOUR TOOLBOX

Open the Manufacturer's handbook

Psychologists say there's a reason for everything we do. We may snap back with a *déjà vu* because of hurts inflicted in the past.

Our Father yearns to break the cycle of hurting people who hurt others. We were never meant to pay back evil for evil. Even in conversation, we are to avoid quarreling. As much as possible, God plans for us to live at peace with one another.

We're blessed with the privilege of serving as an apprentice to the Master Craftsman. He teaches us how to mend the wear and tear caused by those who rub against us the wrong way.

How Can Our Brokenness Be Repaired?

After I've backfired, sputtered and coughed, I sometimes wish God would hit the recall button on my life. Though I'm an older model, I'm confident the Manufacturer could fix me. Since the Creator of the Universe made mankind out of dirt, surely He could tidy up my messed up life. His Word speaks of the availability of Living Water, so why wouldn't it be possible for me to come to Him with freshly washed hands and a clean heart?

We're looking for a fresh bit of faith to climb out of stinky circumstances where we've bogged down. ". . . I tell you the truth, if you have faith as small as a mustard seed, you can say to this mountain, 'Move from here to there,' and it will move. Nothing will be impossible for you" (Matthew 17:20 NIV). Most likely there's a shovel nearby for us to start working on our mountain of problems, one shovel full at a time.

The Devil Made Me Do It

Sometimes we say things without thinking, then cringe, "Why did I say that?" We cast a disapproving glance when our spouse, children or an acquaintance says something that strikes a wrong chord. When someone steps on a tender emotional toe, it can trigger anger or a defensive explosion. We may retaliate with a sarcastic remark that's akin to humor filtered through a screen of bitterness.

Questioning our words and actions isn't unique. The Apostle Paul expressed how perplexed he was by some of his own actions: "What I don't understand about myself is that I decide one way, but then I act another, doing things I absolutely despise" (Romans 7:15 MSG). If Paul, trained and inspired by God, didn't understand some things he did, then why should we be an exception? We target others with put-downs, only to find we've shot ourselves in the foot. I'm not agile enough to kick myself anymore. Though I sometimes say and do dumb things, it's not a proven fact that those things are to define who I am in Christ.

My Cup Overflows

Visualize a person with a storage capacity, a reservoir of self that represents one's entire being. This is a Biblical concept expressed by David in Psalms 23. "My cup overflows." He used the word "cup" in the same way we use the word "reservoir." This spiritual water he speaks of satisfies deep inner dryness that wards off emotional dehydration.

Jesus proclaimed, "You're blessed when you've worked up a good appetite for God. He's food and drink in the best meal you'll ever eat" (Matthew 5:6 MSG). God alone can satisfy the hunger emanating from empty hearts. I wonder why we keep chewing on left-over mistakes when God has prepared a banquet table with the fresh baked bread of life. And He's invited us to come as His honored guest.

In chapter four of the book of John, we find Jesus walking through the countryside with his followers. They stop at a well where the disciples leave Jesus to go into the village to buy food. When a Samaritan woman comes to draw water, Jesus asks her for a drink. He told her if she'd ask, He'd give her Living Water. It was unlike the well water that quenched thirst for only a brief period of time. The water He offered would flow as a bubbling spring—satisfying her spiritual thirst forever.

Full is Fantastic—Drained Is Depressing

The levels in our individual reservoirs fluctuate, like a barometer that moves up or down, depending on how we feel. When we're emotionally full, life is rich—as refreshing as cool water. We become the person God planned for us before we were born. When our emotional needs are met, it frees us to focus on filling the needs of others, with the assurance we won't be drained in the process.

Nothing seems to go right when our reservoirs are dangerously low. No one seems to understand or even like us. We may even have difficulty liking ourselves. The heavy weight of weariness is a burdensome yoke across our shoulders.

We express this empty feeling when we say, "I'm drained." When we get up in the morning, we wish it were night. If we're awake in the middle of the night, we toss and turn, anxiously awaiting the first glimmer of daylight. Satan, the master of deceit, lies on the pillow next to us and whispers, "Your life is a mess. You can't ever do anything right." When we recognize this as one of Satan's conniving schemes, we'll refuse to look for evidence that would validate his lies.

Let the Water Flow

Advertisers work overtime, trying to convince us that buying the latest model of most anything will make us happy. When we give in and purchase the item, we may be excited for a time, but total satisfaction soon leaks away.

A study of those who've won the lottery found that the winners assumed all their problems would be resolved if they threw money at them. However, they frequently found their lives growing more stressful. Family and "friends" contrived ways to get their clutches on a part of the winnings, by hook or crook. The winners were disillusioned by the very people they thought they could love and trust.

In an attempt to fill reservoirs without God, people struggle many ways to excel—in education, in athletics, or perhaps by hoarding wealth. Others climb the corporate ladder and reach the top, only to discover winds of loneliness blowing across, leaving them feeling empty and disheartened.

Fill us Lord—fill this thirsting of our souls, so we can grasp the plan and purpose You have for our lives.

Fill Others—Don't Drain Them

It doesn't make sense that filling others would be more satisfying than filling our own reservoirs. Acts of kindness, however, can create an afterglow that warms us to our toes. When we're walking with God, we don't have to be overly concerned when the recipient doesn't express gratitude for what we've done for them. We'll learn to look for God's approval and discover He's nearby, ready to replenish our supply when it runs low.

When my brother, Sam, three years older than I, was in high school, he wrote an essay entitled, *My Best Friend*. The concluding sentence was: "My best friend is my little sister." That essay has been tucked away for decades, but I get it out occasionally to read it again. I talk to Sam regularly on the telephone, and he continues to offer me refreshing encouragement. He shares my joys and offers a shoulder to cry on when needed. He fills my reservoir.

Reservoirs are filled in different ways. When we discover something a person wants, it's an enriching experience to fulfill that desire. My son thoroughly cleaned the kitchen for his wife on Mother's Day. She reacted with such jubilance; you'd thought he'd bought her an expensive piece of jewelry. Since reservoirs are filled in different ways, it's good to find out what pleases those we love.

Everyone thirsts for the Living Water Jesus offered the woman at the well. As our Father fills us, we become unbroken cisterns— deep wells that never run dry.

Father, teach us how to fill the emptiness in those who are lonely or brokenhearted. Lead us to parched ground that waits to soak up the rain of Living Water.

SCRIPTURES TO CONSIDER

Matthew 17:20
Romans 7:15
Matthew 5:6
Romans 12:17-21

QUESTIONS FOR DISCUSSION

1. If I could start life over again, I would . . .

2. Something I'd like to do now is . . .

3. Today I could work on . . .

4. One thing I can learn from my mistakes is . . .

5. Since Satan is called the *accuser,* how is he accusing me about things I've done or said in the past?

6. A family member I'd like to help is . . .

3

FEED MY HUNGER, QUENCH MY THIRST

What is missing in my life?

In some third world countries, children's tummies hurt because they're hungry. In the United States, ours often hurt because we stuff ourselves or eat too much junk food. Many of us over-indulge by eating at smorgasbords that advertise, "All you can eat."

Jesus referred to himself as the Bread of Life. God planned for our lives to be filled with this non-fattening Bread. Like manna falling from heaven in the wilderness, Jesus makes himself available every day. He, like bread, is our staff of life. We received an invitation to come to the Lord's Table to "taste and see that He is good" (See Psalms 34:8).

Physical and Spiritual Needs

In the movie *What About Bob?* Bill Murray played the part of an emotionally disturbed patient of a psychiatrist, played by Richard Dreyfuss. Bob ultimately drove his psychiatrist crazy. We laughed until we cried when Bob clung to his psychiatrist and pled, "I need, I need, I need."

We require the essential elements of air, water, food, clothing and shelter to remain healthy. It is our responsibility to get proper nutrition, exercise and rest. If these conditions aren't met, health begins to slip away. A person mopes around; the body begins to malfunction and becomes susceptible to disease. If there's no intervention, organs begin to shut down as death sneaks down the alley and knocks at our back door.

On the flip side, we're surrounded by those whose hearts cry out for someone to meet their emotional needs. When our psychological and spiritual supply runs low, our hunger for encouragement may cause us to digress to the point we don't have the strength to fill ourselves—much less others. Whether it's physical or emotional, we suffer when we're running on empty. And ignorance doesn't exempt us from the consequences.

Needs in Marriage

Marriage is a contract with definite commitments and expectations. Ideally, when this contract is kept, it fills the spouse's reservoir. It's draining when either party feels he or she isn't getting what is expected from the marriage.

Further, it's tragic when either hurts the other so deeply and for so long, they both lose the incentive to satisfy the needs of the other.

Whether it is from willful or unintentional neglect, when people fail to satisfy the spiritual or emotional hunger of their spouse, the relationship deteriorates. Scripture tells us: "If you don't do what you know is right, you have sinned" (James 4:17 CEV). That statement doesn't give much wiggle room for us to "weasel out" of our responsibilities.

I heard a beautiful example of a relationship when the husband announced, "I work outside the home to make a living for my family and my wife makes the living worthwhile." An even higher standard is met when each spouse is willing to give his expectations to the Lord. Then, each time one reaches out to the other with kindness, it comes as a pleasant surprise, a bonus that strengthens their relationship.

The Right Diet

When my youngest son, Chip, was nine, he bought a pair of hamsters. He asked me to buy hamster food. Since I was sticking tidbits of food in their cage, I didn't hurry to the pet store, because I thought what I gave them would be sufficient until I got around to buying the proper food.

Sunday morning, Chip stood in the kitchen doorway as I finished preparing breakfast. His downcast countenance caught my attention. I noticed a glint of a tear in his eye. "Mom, both hamsters are dead."

I caught my breath. "I'm so-o-o sorry, Chip, it's my fault."

He turned to walk away and mumbled, "And both their pouches are stuffed full of sawdust." I was appalled. The little creatures died because I failed to make sure they got the proper nutrition hamster food supplied. They chewed on sawdust, but it offered no nourishment. The Lord whispered, "This is a reflection of your life. You're neglecting spiritual nourishment when you grab tidbits of church and scatter a smidgen of good works along the way. You've failed to realize you're starving to death spiritually." This wake-up call shouted, "Reconsider your priorities in life!"

I was aware of basic physical needs, but in skipping through life, I'd neglected spiritual enrichment for myself and my children. I'd not strengthened my relationship with God, nor had I spent quality time teaching my children biblical truths. The impact of this negligence swept over me.

Jabs of "you're so inadequate" drained my emotional tank. Anxiety nipped at my heels and self-condemnation badgered me with accusations. Then, it suddenly dawned on me that this current attitude was as bad as the former—perhaps worse than negligence. It was time to go to the Divine Chiropractor for an attitude adjustment and take care of things in life that were "out of whack."

It's healthy to be conscious of the things we do that give us a spiritual and emotional boost. Often the most enjoyable things include others—either doing something with them or for them. As we fill others, we are filled. The satisfaction goes to a deeper level when we reach out to someone who can't repay us for what we've done. As we serve Christ in this way, with this attitude, we please God, others will be pleased and you can even feel good about yourself.

God's Pure Water

There's almost a magical element in listening to the sound of a stream flowing beside a mountain trail. Water splashing from a waterfall or tumbling over rocks tends to wash away stress. The sound of water creates one of the most peaceful sounds in all nature. Some doctors have an aquarium in their office in hopes it will have a calming effect on patients waiting for an appointment.

The Great Physician provides Living Water to drink, as well as inviting us to come close to Him for a place to rest. Jesus commended anyone who would give a cup of cold water in His name.

My neighbor's little three-year-old daughter came in the living room with a small teacup of water and offered it to one of her mother's friends. Other guests commented about how sweet and thoughtful she was, and asked for their own cup of water. After several trips, the little girl returned and announced sadly, "No more water." Her mother cocked her head and frowned, "What do you mean?" The three-year-old motioned for her mom to follow as she went into the bathroom and pointed to the commode. She could no longer reach the water in the toilet. This is not the kind of water God referenced!

You and I are to avoid contaminated water because we know some water carries the kiss of death. A man adrift on a raft in the ocean knows the danger of drinking salt water. It would not only increase his thirst, but if he drinks it, his body becomes more and more dehydrated. Our Father intends for us to be filled with His provision of Living Water. "May the God of green hope fill you up with joy, fill you up with peace, so that your believing lives, filled with the life-giving energy of the Holy Spirit, will brim over with hope" (Romans 15:13 MSG)!

Where's the Handle on the Faucet?

I remember the first time I ever experienced a sensor on a drinking fountain. I kept looking for the handle and as I bent over to take a closer look, water squirted in my face. My sister-in-law went into the bathroom of a nice restaurant to wash her hands and placed her purse in an adjacent sink where a sensor turned on the water and filled her purse—whoops!

Unfortunately, we have no sensor that automatically turns on Living Water to supply our spiritual and emotional thirst. We must continue to search God's Word to look for the "handle" or the trigger that initiates the spiritual flow that gives us the ability to live an enriched life.

Itching for Answers

My leg itched something awful after a fire ant bit me. I scratched the bump until it almost bled before it dawned on me. "I should put medication on it." When I found a tube of "anti-itch" cream in the medicine cabinet, I applied it and it took care of the itch.

Thousands of people are "itching" to know how to get their spiritual needs met. God's Word tells of the Great Physician, who offers a spiritual balm that cures such longings. His prescription consists of the *Bread of Life* to be taken daily with *Living Water*. How great it is when He delivers both with good bed-side manner.

The Source

We've used "reservoir" as a term that represents a capacity to be filled (or drained) of psychological and spiritual water. The Lord welcomes us to come to the source. "The Lamb on the Throne will shepherd them, will lead them to spring waters of Life. And God will wipe every last tear from their eyes" (Revelation 7:17 NIV). I like to picture the Lord handing me a cup of cool water to quench my thirst. He continues to stand nearby with a pitcher to refill my cup when it runs low.

Lord, fill me until my joy runs over into the lives of others. Send showers of blessings on the dry and thirsty areas in people's lives. Give them the opportunity to soak up Your reign.

SCRIPTURES TO CONSIDER

Psalms 101:2
Romans 15:2
Galatians 6:2
Ephesians 5:28
1 Thessalonians 5:14
Hebrews 10:24

QUESTIONS FOR DISCUSSION

1. One emotional need I have is . . .

2. Needs I have that are common to others are . . .

3. When my reservoir is low, I . . .

4. An emotional need that I have met is . . .

5. To better fill my reservoir or get my emotional needs met, I could . . .

6. To better fill the reservoir or meet the emotional needs of others I could . . .

SECTION II
BASIC NEEDS

4

DON'T YOU RECOGNIZE ME?

Haven't we met before?

Most of us feel awkward when others ignore us, because it conveys the message that we're not important enough to be noticed. We experience a hint of worthlessness when others fail to pay attention to us.

We consider it an honor when a celebrity or a well-known person remembers our name or pays attention to us, although it doesn't have to be someone famous. One of my little grandsons thrilled me when he'd rush into the room and grab me around my knees and squeal, "Momweeze!" Such recognition is more welcome than ice cream on a hot day.

The Apostle Paul wrote, "Love one another with brotherly affection . . . outdo one another in showing honor" (Romans 12:10 RSV). We lift the spirits of others when we compliment them on a job well done. Even flashing a friendly smile sends a message of warm recognition and acceptance.

Jesus was at Bethany in the house of Simon the leper when a woman slipped in with an alabaster jar of expensive ointment. She poured it on Jesus' feet as He "sat" at the table. Several disciples condemned the woman for being wasteful, but Jesus countered their criticism. He acknowledged her loving kindness, assuring her she'd done a beautiful thing.

God Grows Beautiful Flowers

Flowers have wondrous features. Though millions grow far from civilization in the wilderness, I'm confident our Creator enjoys watching the flowers He designed burst into full bloom. "If God gives such attention to the appearance of wildflowers—most of which are never seen—don't you think He'll attend to you, take pride in you, do His best for you" (Matthew 6:30 MSG)?

All of us, like flowers, thrive on "tender loving care." We funnel TLC through praise and appreciation. When we fail to show this kind of love, we pocket the change that could purchase a drink for someone who longs for a tiny sip of appreciation.

Water is indispensible for growth. Driving through parched West Texas sands, one may see only barren waste with an occasional cactus and sagebrush on one side, while across the highway there are lush green fields that thrive because of irrigation water.

Scripture is filled with refreshing references to water. "The Spirit and the bride say, 'Come!'. . .Whoever is thirsty, let him come; and whoever wishes, let him take the free gift of the water of life" (Revelation 22:17 NIV). This water keeps us growing spiritually.

Praise and Appreciation

Praise and appreciation make the personality blossom, just as refreshing water causes a flower to bloom. It's deeply satisfying when others give us sincere praise. And when we praise God, He comes through the door and blesses us with His presence.

If we stood on a street corner with a stack of $5.00 bills with instructions to give one to every person passing by, people might be a bit skeptical, but most would be happy to take the money. As the benefactor, we'd feel good. Suppose, however, that for every $5.00 bill we gave away, we were told to put one in our pocket. Fun! This would more than double the satisfaction.

Perhaps we can't give money away, but we can be generous

with praise and appreciation. It's a satisfying experience when we fill the reservoir of others and discover some of our own needs have been met. That's what we refer to as a win-win situation.

However, praise must be sincere and never overdone. Insincere praise is called *flattery*. It's like sending a flood when people only need a small shower to water their souls. We have a legitimate reason to question flattery, because there have been times when we found ulterior motives couched beneath mushy words.

Address labels tell where a package is to be sent, while the labels people place on us are a factor in determining how far we'll go in life. I didn't praise my children enough. I was afraid they'd become haughty or prideful. I wish I'd realized that the lack of praise squashes healthy self-confidence, as well as stifling their motivation to climb to their highest potential. Perhaps a few individuals become cocky because of an inordinate amount of praise, but many more suffer from a lack of it. Praise should be specific and genuine.

It's sad when we treat people as if there's such a limited supply of praise we ration it. Without praise, personalities wither. When we fail to tell people how much they mean to us or fail to commend them for what they've accomplished, they may conclude we have valid reasons why we don't affirm them. It may make them wonder what's wrong with them.

We don't need critics, we need a cheering section. What a difference it would make if we'd sprinkle a little seasoning of encouragement on those who feel their lives have lost its flavor.

When praise and encouragement are deserved the least, they are often needed the most. If someone is acting at his worst and is difficult to live with, he still needs reassurance that he has redeemable qualities and deserves to be loved.

The father of the prodigal son set a wonderful example. He refused to write his son off. He watched (and I'm sure prayed) for the time when he'd see his son coming down the road toward home. Anyone who has wandered off desperately needs to see yellow ribbons covering the tree in the front yard that shout, "Welcome home!"

Appreciation

Several months back I had a shipment of books arrive by UPS. I rushed out to meet the truck and asked the driver if he'd stack the books on boards I'd laid on the floor in the garage to keep air circulating around them. He graciously agreed. I thanked him a couple of times for doing a good job. Then, I asked him if he'd like something to drink. He declined my offer, but turned with his hand on his chin. "You know, I appreciate the encouragement you gave me, ma'am. Seldom do people ask me to do anything—they *tell* me what to do and when I'm finished, they don't even bother to thank me." How sad. Everyone needs appreciation to refill tanks that are running low—near empty.

I've heard parents say, "I can't understand why my kids turned out the way they did." Couples wonder why they don't have better marriages after years of nit-picking. A solution to better relationships might surface if we looked for opportunities to give genuine praise and appreciation instead of criticism. We could water their flowers, not the weeds.

My friend's son started the school year in a bad way. He was failing in all but one of his classes. His father and mother tried all kinds of discipline and restrictions to motivate him to improve his grades. Nothing worked. Finally, the father decided he'd use a different approach. The next time his fifth-grader brought home a failing paper for him to sign, his dad looked it over and explained that several answers were good. He searched for tiny bits of improvement and congratulated his son. He was thrilled as the boy's grades began to improve. By the end of the year, his son was on the honor roll.

Show Honor to All

"And now friends, we ask you to honor those leaders who work so hard for us, who have been given the responsibility of urging and guiding you in your obedience. Overwhelm them with appreciation and love" (1 Thessalonians 5:12 MSG).

We need to pay attention as to how we treat those around us. Do we shower them with affirmations or pelt them with criticism?

If what we reap comes from what we sow,
Then what we water determines what we grow.

My husband, Carey, ordered hundreds of little embroidered red roses with sticky backs and gave them to people to wear as a reminder to water flowers instead of weeds. He wrote the following poem:

FLOWERS OR WEEDS?

Are you growing flowers or weeds?
It's up to you to choose the seeds.
This applies to personalities too,
And there are things you can do.
If you simply focus on the wrong
Friendship will only last so long.
Assure others of what they've done right,
Refreshing words make their hearts light.
Implore others to do what they can.
Encourage your son to be a man.
Put-downs make people feel dumb.
And criticism makes hearts go numb.
Your words can have a positive flavor,
Words can be tasty, ones they will savor.
If your words take a negative view,
Others aren't likely to listen to you.
Look for success, record that score.
Encouragement spurs them to do even more.
If failures are all one can see,
Self-confidence will soon begin to flee.
When praise is given in full measure
Hearts can receive it as a treasure.
When criticism is all you can spout
You may develop psychological gout.

Touch is an additional way to convey a message of appreciation and approval. Pats on the back and "high fives" are meaningful when cheering others on. Carey told others that our marriage would never be incompatible as long as he had the "income" and I remained "pattable."

Lord, give us the wisdom to know what would be helpful for those around us. Show us what would give them affirmation and support to boost their confidence in order to see them to reach their full potential.

SCRIPTURES TO CONSIDER

Matthew 26:6-13
Romans 12:9-16
Romans 13:8-10
1 Corinthians 13:6
1 Peter 3:7-9

QUESTIONS FOR DISCUSSION

1. My confidence is built when people show me recognition by ...

2. When someone gives me a sincere compliment I ...

3. An insincere compliment makes me feel . . .

4. I would like to show more appreciation to . . .

5. I water weeds when I . . .

6. Three people I could praise for something they have done are:

5

DON'T LEAVE ME ON THE OUTSIDE LOOKING IN

Tell me you want me

In elementary school when leaders were choosing sides, my heart cried out, "Choose me, choose me." I wanted to be needed. I still do. Belonging makes me feel like a child's favorite teddy bear—snuggled and loved.

We yearn for others to care, to know they'll stick with us through bad times as well as good. No one wants to think of themselves as a non-entity. That's why gang members boast, "I'm willing to die for our gang." This solemn commitment is sometimes sealed with blood.

I Belong!

Times were hard. It was a financial strain for my parents to send me to college. On the ill-advice of a relative, I majored in business. Shorthand almost did me in. The faster the pace, the squigglier the characters, that were supposed to represent words. I might as well have tried to transcribe hieroglyphics.

Fearfully, I wrote a letter home. "I'm probably going to fail shorthand—I just can't keep up." I braced myself for my dad's anticipated response, "We're scraping together every penny we can to keep you in college. You buckle down and pass that course."

I went to my mailbox daily, waiting for a scathing letter. The day the letter arrived, my palms were sweaty, and I trembled as I ripped the envelope open and read in disbelief: "Sweetheart, I'm sorry school is so hard for you. But if you fail, you certainly won't be the first—or the last. Just do the best you can, and don't worry about it." Gratitude surfaced in the form of tears because I knew I was loved and still accepted. Failure would not bring down the hammer of rejection.

How the Seed is Planted

Belonging is either strengthened or weakened by the way people treat us. Failure to feel accepted can sometimes hurt to the point that we're devastated. God planned for the family to provide the first evidence of belonging. The process of bonding begins in the womb before a child is born. After birth, if the baby is not loved and cherished, a newborn may suffer from the *Failure to Thrive Syndrome* and even die, though his physical needs have been taken care of.

If a child's need to feel loved isn't met by his family, it's difficult to fill those gaping holes elsewhere. Later, in school or in society, a person may conclude he's never a part of the "in" crowd.

Though this feeling of belonging is essential, a psychological study revealed that one out of three people complained they didn't feel they belonged. This large portion of the population may suffer from disheartening thoughts that pound their minds, "No one really cares. I don't even matter." Their lonely alienation causes them to concede, "I'm living on the outside, looking in."

It takes wisdom to know how to fill the emptiness that sweeps over us when it appears we've been left out. This void can haunt us in the midst of a crowd or when we are alone. The devil sneaks around to convince us we've been alienated and then he attacks us with self-pity. Most of us have feelings of loneliness—especially after we've failed in some way.

Words of criticism, a disparaging tone of voice or a look of disapproval may insinuate that a person is unwanted or looked down on. My sister was self-conscious because our brothers made fun of the size of her feet. When they tried to teach her to dance, they said it was like pushing a wheelbarrow with no tire. It was only after she married a very affirming husband that she overcame these feelings of alienation.

Words of criticism create deep emotional scars on one's self-image. Some continue to look for evidence that they *are* an intrusion in the world. The importance of feeling accepted is evident from the large number of adults who go for counseling because of the rejection they've experienced at some point in their life.

On the other hand, we can reach out in myriads of ways. Smiles, a tender touch, thrown kisses or even a loving glance affirms that "all is right with the world," and someone cares.

What Does Your Family Need?

When people are asked to complete the sentence, "The thing that would help our family the most is . . ." A frequent answer is: "For us to spend more time together." It's easy to become so involved in our individual activities that we fail to keep a close tab on other's needs.

Even when we're together, we tend to be absorbed in a television program or mesmerized while facing the computer. We shut ourselves away from the world with an iPod plugged in our ear. Technology is a factor in limiting more meaningful relationships.

We mustn't be guilty of rationalizing, "it's not the quantity, but rather the quality of time we spend together." It's ridiculous to claim we truly love someone and yet make little or no effort to spend more than bits of our lives with them.

In an attempt to strengthen the family bond, one of my neighbors set aside Friday night as family night. He was shocked when he overheard his son groan, "I wonder what we're going to *have* to do on Daddy's night?" That comment changed the dad's approach. Now, he takes each child out once a month to do whatever that child chooses. This accomplishes his goal and is more satisfying for the children.

When talking to our children, it's important to give them our full attention. We grow close when we detect the heartbeat of their needs. One day our son, Chip, said, "Why is that we have to look at you when you're talking to us and you don't seem to pay attention when we talk to you?"

Ouch!

Our oldest daughter worked as a respiratory therapist at a local hospital. She called home one night. Her voice trembled, "Mom, a lady just died while I was working on her." We had a house full of company and I brushed her off with casual response, "Oh, I'm sorry, honey," and started to hang up the phone.

"Wait, Mom, I need to talk. This is really hard." I apologized because I'd failed to pay attention and listen to her when she needed to work through the trauma she'd just experienced.

Our Children Need Us

I was pursuing an advanced degree and working full-time teaching while struggling to take care of the necessary chores around home. My youngest son, Chip, was in junior high and didn't seem to care where I was or what I was doing.

However, one night he came into the kitchen while I was preparing supper and hopped up on the counter. "Mom, I wish you'd have another baby." (There was no way this was on my want list!) I grimaced, "Chip, I think I've had my quota." He countered with, "Then why don't we adopt a baby?" I looked at him in amazement while he continued, "Mom, you're never home." My mouth dropped open as I realized he *did* miss me when I wasn't around. He'd reasoned that I'd likely stay home more if I had a baby to care for.

The Power of a Moment's Attention

A church deacon put on his coat and was ready to leave for an important meeting when his six-year-old came to him with a picture of his class and held it up for his dad to see. "Daddy, look at this." His dad glanced at the picture briefly and mumbled something about it being a good-looking bunch of kids and handed it back. His son took the picture, but dropped his head as a look of dejection spread across his face. "Daddy, don't you want to hear their names?"

Here was a conflicting situation. A church member was outside in the car waiting to take the dad to an important meeting, and the boy's father had little or no interest in learning the names of these children. However, the sad expression on his little boy's face prompted him to make a quick decision. He sent an older child out to tell his friend to go on, he'd join him later. He sat down in his overstuffed chair, took his child on his lap and listened as his son pointed to every single student in the photo and called each by their first and last names. His daddy hugged him. "Wow, son—that was great!"

His son beamed. "Bet you thought I couldn't do it." Then he jumped down and ran off to play. What a good feeling this father had as he left to attend his meeting. He knew he'd made the right decision.

The feeling of belonging is filled in different ways by different individuals. It may become the motivation to join certain clubs or groups. It leads people to seek membership with those who have common interests. Professional organizations and honor societies attract those with similar goals. Membership and fellowship in a church often fulfill the need to belong. God tells us: "let us not neglect our meeting together, but encourage one another . . ." (Hebrews 10:25 NLT).

Whether in a political group or a football team, the world searches for things to be a part of. It's a satisfying way of saying, "Me, too." It is a rare individual who chooses to live as a hermit because he doesn't want to be around people.

Though the yearning to belong can be strong at all ages, it appears to peak during adolescent years. Inner-city gangs are formed for this purpose. School spirit and loyalty supplement this desire. Peer pressure can wield much more power over teens than parental influence.

Teenage years seem to swoop down overnight when the generation gap suddenly widens to a deep chasm. The typical complaint from a teen is, "Nobody else's parents . . ." or "everyone else gets to. . ." Psychologists assure us that if a child has a strong feeling of acceptance from his parents, he's less likely to succumb to peer-pressure.

A Square or a Chicken?

Pressure to abide by specific rules is exerted by some social groups. Methods may vary and consequences altered, but group acceptance plays a strong part in shaping our lives. Possibly it reaches its zenith in the mafia, where a person is ostracized or even "bumped off" if he doesn't stick to the rules. Members are coerced by threats and ultimatums that create a fear of what will happen if they don't do as they're told.

In school, ridicule and teasing force young people to conform. Even when a child knows his behavior is socially unacceptable, he may feel the pressure to "fall in line" and live up to the demands of his circle of friends. Such terms as "square, chicken or yellow" are used to cause boys and girls to do everything from drugs to driving at dangerous speeds.

In high school, we played a dangerous game with two cars filled with teenagers. One driver would speed down a narrow dirt road toward the other, to see which car would swerve into the ditch in order to keep from crashing head-on. We called it "Chicken." Now, I call it "Stupid."

The consequences change from time to time, but pressure is still exerted to squeeze people into molds. Hearing the word, "cool" can cause a young person to ignore the possible consequences of their actions. Teens sometimes develop a misguided mindset that they're young and invincible. Some disregard the biblical principle that one reaps what he sows. Caution may be thrown to the wind when a young person seeks a bit of acceptance and the assurance that he belongs.

On the Other Hand

In the delightful play, "Fiddler on the Roof," tradition played a powerful role in controlling the way Jewish people lived. Customs, traditions and *mores* are still used to force others to conform and control certain behaviors. Today, young people often belittle tradition with the comment, "Times have changed. We don't live in the dinosaur age." It's no compliment to be accused of living in the dark ages.

Tradition can elevate honor and dignity. It can also shackle and dampen growth and progress. Customs can lay a foundation for respect and love or they become a blanket that smothers insight, logic, or truth.

Fashion, Fad, or Foolishness

A podiatrist reported that when women's shoe fashions featured pointed toes and high spiked heels, his business almost tripled. Women came to him complaining that their feet hurt. After examining a patient, he'd explain there was nothing physically wrong with her feet, and he'd suggest that she get rid of the poorly designed shoes she was wearing. Too often the response was, "I can't throw these away. They're the latest style. Besides, they cost a lot of money!" The foot doctor would roll his eyes, massage her feet to give temporary relief, and suggest she come back in a couple of weeks.

New styles are introduced as a motivation for people to purchase the latest fad as evidence they belong. It alarmed me when the news reported a teen murdered a classmate in order to steal his name-brand athletic shoes.

One woman told me she went to garage sales in classy neighborhoods to look for expensive name-brand clothes. She buys articles of clothing, takes them home, removes the labels and sews them in her daughter's clothes. All this is done so her teenager will feel important.

My granddaughter once begged for a particular brand of jeans. Her mother set a limit on the amount she could spend on school clothes. She said if she wanted the more expensive brand, she'd have to cut back on other articles of clothing or else earn money to pay the difference. It's interesting, because this same granddaughter now dresses in styles that are creative and original. She takes pride in being a non-conformist. She even made a skirt out of her dad's discarded neckties.

Having a depression-day mentality, I'm prone to brag on how *little* I pay for an item. I'm totally unaware of brand names. It didn't bother me that no one cared for the style of furniture we had when we first married. We called the boxes, crates, and make-dos, "early matrimonial."

We may not appreciate some styles. My brother-in-law disliked neckties because he said they choked him, but his job required him to wear them. When they sang the song at church, *Bless Be The Tie That Binds,* he said he almost croaked.

An Answer to a Need

Perhaps one of the reasons God established the church was for Christians to experience a sense of belonging as they work together. The Bible tells us we are all parts of the body of Christ, and each has a different purpose. There's something missing when a member fails to do his part.

We were meant to support one another emotionally. Because we care for the rest of the body, when one has sorrow, we all grieve; when one rejoices, we're all happy. Some stop going to church because they don't feel they belong. They may have gone to a church that has been compared to cold butter—which doesn't spread very well.

If every visitor in church were met with a sincere smile, welcomed and cared for, this sense of "not belonging" could disappear.

It's possible this could be the key to our churches being filled and bulging at the seams.

Seek First

A strong bond with God and His unprecedented acceptance causes all other aspects of belonging to pale into insignificance. "Seek ye first the kingdom of God and His righteousness, and all these things will be added unto you" (Matt. 6:33 NIV). Our Father promises He'll never leave or forsake us. This gives us strong assurance that we belong to Him.

It takes my breath away to think that God actually sacrificed His own Son in order for us to be a part of His family. "See, I have engraved you on the palms of my hand" (Isaiah 49:16 NIV). When He engraved me on His hand, He put me in a place where He could hold me tight.

Lord, not only do I want to belong, but I want to help others know they belong. Give me enough love to embrace the unlovable and to comfort those who are lonely.

SCRIPTURES TO CONSIDER

Hebrews 10:25
Romans 12:4,5
Ephesians 4:25
Matthew 6:33
Isaiah 49:16

QUESTIONS FOR DISCUSSION

1. Do you feel you have a strong sense of belonging in your family? Explain

2. Our family would feel a greater sense of belonging if. . .

3. The group or organization in which I feel a sense of belonging to is. . .

4. I experience great fellowship with other Christians when . . .

5. I can help others feel they belong by. . .

6. What do you think it implies when scripture says God has engraved us on the palm of His hand?

6

SAFE AND SECURE

Oh, no! My security blanket is in the laundry

Security is closely related to touch. In a strange way, the more insecure we feel, the tighter we like to be held. God intends for us to feel safe and secure as he wraps His arms around us. When there's no one else available, we may cross our arms and squeeze our own shoulders. My mom suggested I wrap my tiny babies tight in their blankets, so they'd feel snug and secure. She reminded me, "In the womb they've been confined to a small space for months before being thrust into a wide open world."

When a small child doesn't feel safe, he may be reluctant to trust others enough to become involved in social activities. He makes this obvious when he hides in the folds of his mother's skirt when others speak to him. It takes time and a positive environment for an insecure person to trust those outside his comfort zone.

Each fall, at the beginning of the school year, there are children who are frightened at the thought of their mothers leaving them behind in kindergarten. My niece experienced this when she attempted to drop her five-year-old off at school. Naomi cried and clung to her mother, begging her not to leave. The principal came in, took the child on his lap, leaned over and spoke softly, "Naomi, look at all the other children in the classroom who've let their mothers leave and they're not crying. How do you think they do that?" Naomi wailed louder, "They don't have *my* mother!"

Hunger and Insecurity

A lack of food in third-world countries will cause many to feel insecure about where their next meal is coming from. This is also true in some sectors of our own society, especially the homeless, who live on streets and under bridges.

My friend, Sammie, went bankrupt after being a multi-millionaire. She lived in a shed for several months with no bath, running water or kitchen. Her encounter with poverty stirred her compassion and concern for the homeless. She now spends most of her time, and whatever money she can scrape together to feed the hungry.

My husband, Carey, lost his father when he was twelve. His mother had five children, one only six weeks old. After we married, it took some time for me to understand why Carey always bought far more groceries than we needed. It irritated me, because I had difficulty finding places to store the excess food. Finally, I realized his family had lost their breadwinner when he was young and there were times when they didn't have enough to eat. His insecurity carried over from a time when he'd experienced hunger pains. He still had an underlying fear of having to go without food.

Few Americans today are concerned about a lack of food. Most of our pantries are chocked full. (However, I can feel insecure if I don't have a stash of chocolate chip cookies stuck back for emergencies.) We can be picky, but not panicky, because we have plenty to eat. A sensible friend suggested we don't really need something to eat if we're not hungry enough to eat an apple.

Secure and Safe

Our personal security is slanted toward ways of staying safe. It's been years since we could leave our houses unlocked or the keys in our cars. In my childhood, we didn't own keys to our home. We never lost the car keys, because they were always left in the ignition.

Today, parents become fearful when their children are out of their sight, even in their own back yard. My niece sold her home when she learned that a child molester had moved next door. She had a valid reason for her concern about the safety of her eight children.

The loss of identity can be even more unsettling than the loss of money. It's disconcerting to know there are devices that are able to read credit card information through our purses and wallets. All the more now, we know our only true security comes from staying close to our Father. We identify Him as our strong tower of protection. He watches over every detail of our lives, listens to every whisper of anxiety and monitors our every heartbeat. A blink of an eye is not hidden from His sight.

Do I Have Enough?

Many in our generation are scrambling for more, leading us to believe *things* and *stuff* are essential for financial security. Don't we miss the point if we only seek jobs and occupations that offer the biggest salaries rather than in serving the most people? The Master taught us that if we gain the whole world, yet lose our own soul, we have failed. The value of our contribution to life is not based on our monetary worth.

There may be times when we have to decide which is more important; to make a living or make a difference.

Of course, it's legitimate and sensible to look for a job that includes fringe benefits and insurance. Job security and retirement plans are part of a good package. However, even with large incomes, too many approach the end of each month unable to pay off their credit card debts. And sad to say, many purchases are the result of impulse buying. "Shop 'til you drop" is an indication of the mentality of some. This lifestyle overshadows the benefits of a well-paying "dream job."

Nelson Mandela left a great example. When he found himself at the cross-roads of life, one path led to personal gain and the other to serving his people. He chose the more difficult, but higher calling to help others.

Health

It's reasonable to want good health so we can work and be financially secure. Good nutrition, physical fitness and regular physical examinations are a part of the plan. We give a sigh of relief when our doctor gives us a clean bill of health.

A number of years ago, *Reader's Digest* featured an article each month about some disease or health problem. Immediately following the issue, the doctors found their offices jam-packed with thousands who'd self-diagnosed themselves with the "disease of the month." The magazine made a wise decision when they discontinued that series.

Financial Security

Lottery tickets appeal to those thinking they're on to an effortless way to become rich. A recent jackpot bonanza found people standing in line for hours in order for the most miniscule chance to win. A carpenter working at my home was ecstatic when he won $50 with a lottery ticket. I probably burst his bubble when I asked, "How many hundreds of dollars did you spend to get that one winning ticket?"

Drugs, tranquilizers and alcohol lure those who seek a way to mask their anxieties. These can lead to addictions with their false sense of well-being. Their problems still lurk in the shadows, waiting to taunt them when the effect of the drugs wear off. Our real solution revolves around the One who's able to still the roaring sea as well as the turmoil in our hearts.

Who Is to Blame and Where Do We Go?

One of the saddest insecurities for children is the tragedy of a broken home. With few exceptions, divorce "punches holes in children's reservoirs," allowing their feelings of security to be drained. It's not unusual for children to blame themselves for the divorce, assuming they must have done something wrong to cause the family to fall apart. Divorce is a hurricane that all too often blows an entire family off its foundation. Following the schism, the home is no longer a secure place for parents or children.

Emotional security bonds through friendship. Friends offer support when the rug has been pulled out from under us. A trusted friend warms our hearts when the world has been cold and uncaring. Friendship, like a warm blanket, wraps around us when the winds of adversity have chilled us to the bone.

We gain a feeling of emotional security in good church fellowship, as we interact with our spiritual brothers and sisters. Since we're all a part of God's blood-bought family, we have an obligation to care for one another. Small groups offer even tighter bonding. But watch out, Satan wants to rob us of one of our greatest support systems. When Christians get too busy, they become less involved in one another's lives.

Better Than FDIC

We wouldn't put our money in a bank if we weren't sure it was safe. We check to see if the institution is a member of the Federal Depositors Insurance Corporation. However, God is our FDIC—the **F**ather's **D**ependability **I**n **C**risis. There can be no greater security than to know we can bank on His love, to know He's committed to provide everything that is essential in caring for us. "And my God will meet all your needs according to His glorious riches in Christ Jesus" (Philippians 4:19 NIV). He is Jehovah Jireh, our provider. We are loved and cared for.

My lack of faith is evident when I raise my hands in an attempt to release my problems to the Lord—only to pull them back when I think of one more thing I could try. *Lord, give me the faith to keep my grubby little hands off those things I need to release to You and trust Your wisdom and grace to do what is best.*

Hold Me Tight, Never Let Me Go

Scripture reminds us that every single person messes up and falls short of the Father's glory.

We're relieved to know God never refuses to accept us as His children even when we're confident we'll never qualify as good enough to be adopted as one of His own.

We find life-changing relief when we check our account and find the Holy Spirit made a deposit on our behalf when we committed our lives to Jesus. "Take your everyday, ordinary life—your sleeping, eating, going-to-work, and walking-around life—and place it before God as an offering . . .You'll be changed from the inside out" (Romans 12:1-2 MSG). *Lord, keep me from wiggling out of your hands because I'm bent on doing my own thing.*

God Has His Eye on Us

When we lived in Indiana, we had an enclosed balcony outside our bedroom that we converted into a guest bedroom. It was separated from our room with only curtained French doors. One Sunday morning I stood in my underwear in the middle of the bedroom, dressing for church. A visiting preacher, who'd been sleeping on the balcony, began to sing, "There's an all-seeing eye watching you." I jumped and ran into the closet to finish getting dressed.

I'm so thankful I don't have to jump and run when I realize God has His eye on me. He looks at me in the light of what I can be, not what I've been or done. He saw me before I was dressed or had my hair combed and with no make-up. He even saw the smudges of sin I hadn't gotten around to cleaning off my conscience through confession.

What Are You Doing With What God Has Given You?

When I accept how much the Lord has invested in me, I can go to the bank and cash the check. It's been signed by God, endorsed by Jesus and notarized with the seal of the Holy Spirit. This Savings Account gives me the resources to live the abundant life God has reserved for me. It is a culmination of His wisdom, guidance, peace and joy. He pays high dividends for the comparatively small investment I made by giving my life to Him.

God promises the kind of security that's not available through any other realm. "The One who died for us . . .is in the presence of God at this very moment sticking up for us . . ." (Romans 8:35 MSG). Genuine security is to know trouble, hard times, sickness and even death can never drive a wedge between us and our Father. With renewed confidence I sing, "Blessed assurance, Jesus is mine. O what a foretaste of glory divine."

I want us to be able look into the eyes of the One who created us and know we matter because of the beautiful plan He orchestrated for our lives. The presence of Jesus within us is our guarantee that He really will give us all that He promised; and the Spirit's seal upon us gives us more reason to praise our glorious heavenly Father.

Blessed Peace

> Can I be secure and still stand strong
>> When winds of adversity sweep along?
> Will I hold steady with times adverse?

Continue to praise God—rather than curse?
I'll hold God's hand for security within
Then face the future, knowing I'll win!
LLL

I'm convinced God is not so much concerned about what happens to us here as He is about *how* we respond to things we experience. Our security is based on our belief that He is powerful enough to walk us through all seasons of life and into triumphant victory.

We're amazed by a man who is totally blind, but develops other God-given abilities to compensate and successfully navigate his way through life. How incredible that a quadriplegic can stay pleasant and upbeat as she develops her talents in spite of her extreme handicap. God gives us the wisdom to adapt when some of our faculties are weakened or destroyed.

Thank you, Lord. Just as a loving father carries his child, You are more than willing to pick us up when we are weary. Give us a grateful heart for this tender-loving care.

SCRIPTURES TO CONSIDER

Mark 8:36
Philippians 4:19
Romans 12:1–2
Ephesians 1:14

QUESTIONS FOR DISCUSSION

1. I feel secure when. . .

2. It makes me feel insecure when. . .

3. Do you sometimes feel you have needs that aren't supplied? Why do you think this happens? . . .

4. In order for God to transform my mind, I . . .

5. Even when things go wrong, I remember God is still in control because . . .

6. The person I think of who has held steady in the midst of a difficult trial is . . . Explain.

7

HIGH STANDARDS
AND GOALS

Scoring touchdowns in life

If a person telephones to tell me they'd like to come to my house for a visit and they don't have a GPS, my question is: "Where are you coming from?" Though I'd like to give them a round about way to give me a chance to clean house, I usually have second thoughts and give clear directions to my home. In reference to goals, it's important to know where we are and where we want to go.

Near the top of our list for goals in life should be a plan as to how we can be a blessing to others. A phone call, a note, a cheerful word to a clerk or a friendly wave or smile at the mailman can make a difference for that individual.

God didn't provide boot straps with which to pull ourselves up. But every day He lays out the right tools for us to construct things of value so we can build on Jesus' foundation. We follow an extraordinary God who leads us to heights we'd never achieve alone.

Making Goals a Reality

By nature, we're goal-oriented. We observe this in small children when they learn to ride a bicycle or build something with Legos. Deep within, there's a stirring that yearns for something that gives us the satisfaction of accomplishment. It's like an oasis in the desert— whispering for us to come and quench our thirst. Goals are like an unseen hand motioning for us to follow till we reach satisfying waters of fulfillment. We're assured that when we arrive at each personal goal, we'll find a pool to fill a bucket of our needs.

A goal-less life would be as pointless as a goal-less basketball court. If there's no ways to score, there's no occasion for a celebration—no victory. Without a clear purpose, we may well bump into walls or move aimlessly in various directions. Questions such as, "What's the use?" can haunt us.

It's helpful to be a part of a group that works toward similar goals. In groups like AA and Weight Watchers, each lifts the other up with encouragement that gives them the incentive to hold steady.

Surveys have found that only five percent of us have specific goals. If we simply sit, waiting to see which way the wind blows, we may drift in directions it would be best to avoid. This may be a time to get off the fence and start walking. There is a trite but true axiom, "A journey of a thousand miles begins with one step."

Helen Keller's teacher, Ann Sullivan, worked tirelessly and "willed" Helen to be successful in learning to speak. At times, this goal appeared to be impossible, but Ann's remarkable dedication and Helen's tenacity helped them reach this high goal. Helen not only learned to speak, but became an inspiration as she talked to audiences of thousands.

Typically, it's best to share our goals, but there are times when it may be better to keep quiet. In Genesis, Joseph told his brothers what God had shown him in dreams, of his family bowing down to him.

It's understandable why this triggered jealousy and anger among his brothers. When he shared his dreams, they took it as prideful arrogance. However, God accomplished His purpose for him in spite of the cruel treatment his brothers put him through when they sold him into slavery and then lied about it.

Joseph suffered a number of years of hardship and betrayal. But following his time in prison, he was elevated as next in line to Pharaoh. Because of forgiveness, he made the choice to rescue his father and brothers from starvation. With godly insight, he explained that the things his brothers had planned for evil, God used for good.

Seek God's Wisdom in Making Goals

When God becomes the standard of our goal-setting, He opens doors at appropriate times. He gives us discernment, so we're aware of the best time to step into a new experience. His timing is of upmost importance. We flirt with complications when we attempt to force doors open too soon or linger too long before moving forward. The time that we wait is a prime time to pray for guidance. But on the other hand, we must be sure we aren't bound and shackled with procrastination.

Generally, goals should be realistic, but occasionally, God gives visions beyond any hopes or dreams we might have. Think of how outlandish God's promise of a baby must have seemed to Abraham—considering his age and the age of his wife, Sarah. I wonder if God chuckles when He plans things that don't fit into our reasoning or realm of possibilities.

The president of a major steel corporation agreed to pay employees for ideas that would help the business operate more efficiently. This motivated his employees to scratch their heads to think of creative ways to help the company reach its goals. One young man was given $25,000 for his suggestion on a better way to do marketing. We too may benefit by asking wise friends how they believe we should pursue our goals.

Short, Mid and Long-Range Goals

When we're spread too thin, we become distracted and can't focus on any one thing. It's like trying to juggle too many balls at a time. Eventually, we get worn out, drop some of the balls or quit altogether. It's akin to being the "jack of all trades and good at none."

It is wise to set short-range, mid-range and long-range goals. Short-range goals can be compared to first base, made for a week or a month. (Those who are overcoming addictions may need to set hourly goals.) Someone who is attempting to lose weight is advised to hold off at least ten minutes before indulging in a food that tempts him. In that short period, the temptation usually begins to subside or may even go away.

Think of mid-range goals as second base—from three to twelve months. Long-range goals are represented by third base—headed for home. These may stretch from two to twenty years.

A common error is to set short-range goals too high and long-range goals too low. If short-range goals are set too high, we won't be able to reach them. This is likely to "jab a hole" in our self-confidence. If long-range goals are set too low, mediocrity may be the result, as well as unutilized gifts and talents.

Considered alone, long-range goals may appear too lofty, especially if we don't consider all the tiny steps in between. Losing 50 pounds may seem unrealistic, but if we commit to lose one pound at a time, the goal isn't unreasonable. My husband, Carey, didn't help me much when I wanted to lose weight. He shrugged, "Just more to love. Remember, I promised to love you through thick or thin."

In pursuing a goal, there are plateaus when nothing seems to be happening. This calls for a time to persevere. Dissect your goals to find at least one aspect that can be reached short-term. Don't expect much to happen overnight. Pursuing a goal may have spurts and stops—or three steps forward, two steps back. Unrealistic expectations are like the foolishness of praying, "Lord, give me patience and give it to me right now!"

There is the danger of looking so far into to the future that we stumble over opportunities our Father lays at our feet today. In our lack of understanding, the things God places right in front of us may not seem to have anything to do with reaching our goal. In the whole process, learn to check with Him regularly.

Tacking

Because circumstances change, goals should be re-evaluated intermittently. The goals I have at this age are different from those I had fifteen to twenty years ago. Just as a sail boat needs to tack (or zigzag) due to contrary winds, it's often necessary to alter our course rather than continue in a straight line toward our goal. We review our goals periodically; to be assured we're still headed in the right direction. (If we stay on God's course and have Jesus on board, Satan can't sink our boat.) In Acts 16, the Holy Spirit changed Paul's direction four times before he reached his God-given destination. His goal was clear, but his route was altered by the Holy Spirit.

Make Plans

Accomplishing a difficult task is rewarding, especially if we face a chore we've dreaded. It's a good idea to ask God to give us a joyful spirit that is an asset as we tackle hard jobs. A good attitude is powerful in accomplishing difficult tasks. How comforting to know that the Holy Spirit is at work to renew our minds. (See Ephesians 4:23).

It helps for me to wake up with the declaration, "This day belongs to the LORD! Let's celebrate and be glad today"(Psalms 118:24 CEV). I get up early and pour a cup of coffee. It's an opportunity for me to sit alone and have some quiet time—to welcome God to become the focal point of my life. I read and journal. Then, I make out my "to do" list for the day.

Some chores are broken into fifteen minute increments or even smaller bits of time. It's challenging to zip around quickly and tackle big jobs, segmenting bits in small units of time. For example, I make my bed, dress and check my e-mail while making my coffee in the morning. I can wipe off the cabinets during a television commercial.

For years, I kept the skeleton of this book in the closet. My husband worked on it years ago. Though he's been out of the picture for over two decades, I had a desire to accomplish a goal he started. Periodically, I'd pull his material out and struggle to rewrite it.

Recently, I went back again to dig out his dusty notes from the back of the closet to wrestle with a redo. A few mornings later, I woke up with a thought that I believe came from the Lord. "You're trying to write the book in his voice—that won't work. Use your own voice." This nudge came as a blessed prodding, after which, the ideas began to flow. God may someday reveal how many times He tried to let me in on this secret.

A Lesson from History

Toynbee, a famous English historian, traced the great civilizations of mankind through the ancient cultures of the Egyptians, Greeks and Romans. He found they had a common challenge—they all struggled to exist. It is sobering to know his study concluded that each great nation began to crumble when they reached their goals and in a figurative way, sat down to gloat over their accomplishments.

Man is at his best when he is climbing, rather than just sitting on top of the mountain, freezing to death because he's lingered too long planting his flag and taking in the view. Sam Ewing coined a famous quotation: "On the plains of hesitation bleach the bones of countless millions, who, at the dawn of victory, sat down to wait, and in waiting—died." Can you hear the beat of that distant drummer who sets the cadence for your walk with the Lord?

Kinds of Goals

1. Personal—God assures us He'll give us the desires of our heart. But it's our obligation to be sure our desires line up with His.

2. Family— Work on your goals together. A large family saved over a period of years in order for them to build an extra bathroom. Each time they got near their goal, they'd decide they'd rather take a vacation. They laughed at a family reunion years later when they all concluded they'd made a good decision, because of the fun and memories created on the trips they'd taken.

Goals Can Cover Several Areas:

1. Vocational—After we opened our retreat center, one of the board members called the staff together and divided us into groups of four. He asked each group to write down what they envisioned as goals for the center. After a designated period of time, he called the staff back together and wrote our lists on a white board. Everyone was surprised at how different each group perceived those goals. It became obvious that we needed to be on the same page with those we were to work with.

2. Financial—many who have a problem with their finances often have difficulty understanding how their money slips away from them. Those who are successful in handling their money keep a budget or at least check the pulse of their bank account to know where their money is going. A man may be shocked when he analyzes his credit card bills and canceled checks. He may discover he's been pouring money down a

"rat-hole" that accomplishes little of what he really wants. Be aware, wise money managers make sure their gift to the Lord comes off the top.

3. Spiritual—Our long-range goal for heaven must be loud and clear. Short-term and intermediate goals must take into consideration the spiritual direction we're committed to follow. Our primary goal should be to live a life that reflects the indwelling of Jesus and the guidance of the Holy Spirit.

Misplaced goals may be influenced by movies, television programs or from people we hang out with. If there are children in the family, it would be interesting to ask them what they believe are the most important things in their parent's lives.

The secret to goal-setting lies in the Apostle Paul's writings. "Not that I have already obtained all this, or have already arrived at my goal, but I press on to take hold of that for which Christ Jesus took hold of me" (Philippians 3:12 NIV). It's encouraging to know Jesus has already fought many of our battles and we have the opportunity to take hold of the things He has laid aside for us to accomplish.

Lord, let me make it my goal in life to be a blessing to at least one person every day.

SCRIPTURES TO CONSIDER

Matthew 6:33
Colossians 3:1
Philippians 3:12–14

QUESTIONS FOR DISCUSSION

1. The things I'd like to accomplish in my lifetime are . . .

2. The most important goals I want to achieve in the next twelve months are listed below:

PERSONAL GOALS
In the next week –
In the next month –
In the next six months –
In the next year –

Repeat the above steps for the areas of:

3. FAMILY GOALS

4. VOCATIONAL GOALS

5. FINANCIAL GOALS

6. SPIRITUAL GOALS

7. The biggest problem I have in goal setting is . . .

8. From going through the process of goal setting, I learned
   . . .

8

THE THRILL OF ADVENTURE
Climb the highest mountain

All too soon after the last bell marks the end of the school year, many children begin to grumble, "I'm bored." A lack of schedules and inactivity locks those of us who are adults into ruts of "same song, second verse," or as some express it, "same-o, same-o."

A rut is defined as *a grave with the ends kicked out.* We need adventure to get a taste of the spice of life. It can be referred to as the "Tabasco sauce," to add a little zest to the humdrum of our daily existence.

Adventure normally involves something new and challenging. We may get vicarious pleasure going to a science fiction movie or watching a ball game. But it's far better to actively engage in a challenge—to "rev up" the engines of excitement while utilizing our own skills and abilities.

Thank goodness, adventure doesn't require everyone to claw up the side of a rugged cliff. Sheer terror doesn't call my name anymore. When I was young and foolish, my friends and I occasionally went to the graveyard and told horror stories that scared me out of my wits. I should've realized that fear infiltrates our lives and can become a habit that keeps us on edge. I finally asked Jesus to come and "in habit" my life and help me deal with my irrational fears.

The Adventure of Children
We gave birth to what Carey called "quadruplets the hard way"—one a year. In desperation, when I asked him how many children he wanted, he sighed, "I hope I want all of them."

My obstetrician gave my husband some wonderful advice. He told him to get a baby sitter and take me out once a week. He warned him, "You can either choose to spend money on a baby sitter or spend it on doctor bills and medication for your wife." Going out gave me a sense of adventure—something to look forward to and a break from the stress of caring for four little ones.

Adventure leaps into reality when we deliberately choose to do something different or difficult. The choice doesn't have to be costly or complicated. Creativity can conjure up an idea that constitutes an adventure. My quartet of little ones enjoyed hanging a sheet over a card table and pretending it was a tent where they could eat a picnic lunch in their secret hideaway.

Children are typically not as intimidated as most adults. My three–year-old granddaughter began dancing in the aisles at church during praise and worship one Sunday—totally oblivious to the crowd. It was fun for her and thrilled those of us who watched.

When we lived in Colorado Springs, our son Paul was three. Carey was preaching one Sunday and quoted the passage about worshipping in Spirit and truth. He paused briefly to emphasize his point, "Now get this, there are two elements here." Paul sat several rows in front of me and turned and shouted, "Hey, Mom, did you hear that? Dad says there are two elephants here!" I wanted to pretend I didn't know who that little boy belonged to. But he was so excited about having a wonderful adventure in church, he made me laugh.

Challenge is an Adventure

Challenges spark adventure. Wilma Rudolph was one of twenty-two children, born into a poor black family. As a child, she was crippled and in braces until she was nine. When she was twelve, she tried out for basketball, but failed to make the team. The next year, she practiced every day and was chosen for the starting line-up. A college track coach spotted her, saw her potential, and offered her a track scholarship at Tennessee State University.

Wilma made the U.S. Olympic team in 1960. There she faced the world record holder, Jutta Heine, of Germany. Wilma outran her to win both the 100 and the 200-meter sprint. The third race was a relay, where she faced Jutta again. When she reached for the baton, it slipped from her hand and dropped to the ground, giving her German competitor the lead. With stoic determination, Wilma swept the baton from the track and took off in desperate pursuit. In the last few strides of the race, she pulled ahead and won her third gold metal. Her incredible accomplishment was an inspiration for everyone who cheered for her.

The Adventure of the Christian Life

The Christian life is far more than sitting quietly in worship with folded hands. First-century Christianity proved such an adventure that fishermen were willing to drop their nets to follow Jesus. This kind of commitment should challenge us to get out of the boat of mediocrity and follow the Lord. It is a thrill to hear Him invite us, like the enticing call in the Song of Solomon, "Come away with me."

I found it an adventure to go to a Communist country to teach in an underground Christian school. Most of the students there were young adults willing to risk being arrested and thrown in prison in order to learn how to be a servant for the Creator of the Universe and to study His Word. One of the girls in class had just been released from jail for worshipping God. Evidently she'd been treated horribly, because when I asked her to tell me about it, she put her hands over her face, bowed her head and shook it vigorously. Still, the invitation to follow Jesus was forceful enough for her to risk facing further consequences because of her hunger to learn more about how to live as a child of the King.

Being led by God's Holy Spirit may lead one into unforgettable experiences. It's like being blindfolded by a trusted friend and agreeing to follow him wherever he chooses to lead. Now, that's an adventure! We can't predict what doors the Spirit will open when He whispers for us to come. Jesus told the woman at the well that true worshippers must worship in Spirit and in truth. We experience this wonder when truth catapults from our head into our heart. It's equivalent to discovering that someone sprinkled gold dust over Truth to make it sparkle with life-giving Spirit.

Adventure in Serving God

At this writing, my niece is a missionary in an anti-Christian nation. When her team heard authorities were coming to search their house, they buried their Bible materials in the back yard. This scary sense of adventure was a risk these soldiers for Christ were willing to take, because they are on a mission for God Himself.

Worship can be stimulating and exciting. Perhaps it's not in a traditional church building, but beside a lake, on top of a mountain or around a campfire. It can be spontaneous as we watch God move in mysterious, even miraculous ways. A splendid sunset embraces me with God's Holy presence.

When I was in college, a visiting missionary spoke in chapel, and my heart was so moved, I gave him all the money I had. Shocked at what I'd done, I almost scrambled down the aisle to chase the collection plate when I realized I had nothing left to eat on—not even enough for bus fare to go to and from work.

The next day, I received an unexpected check from my dad for double the amount I'd given the missionary. It was a beautiful faith-building adventure when God rewarded me. "Give, and it will be given to you. A good measure, pressed down, shaken together and running over . . ." (Luke 6:38 NIV). In my adventure of trusting God, I received a hundred-fold from my investment.

Other Aspects of Christian Adventure

Fellowship is a part of adventure. My husband and I went to Europe and visited many wonderful places. We went to Rome, Venice, Florence, Paris and Amsterdam. Though the places were wonderful, the greatest adventure for me came about when we met and fellowshipped with Christians in each city. We experienced an instant bonding because we were one in Spirit. We treated one another as if we were long-lost brothers and sisters.

Another aspect of adventure is serving or sharing with others. One of my friend's family members took all her money to go Christmas shopping. She'd just started to shop when someone stole her billfold. My heart grieved. I gave my friend $50 to pass on to her as a token of my concern. My friend said her sister responded, "I'm overwhelmed. I can't remember anyone ever giving me anything before." How sad.

A generous man went to a large department store a few weeks before Christmas and paid off all the gifts people had in lay-away. It was a beautiful surprise for the recipients and an adventure for the benefactor. It's good to periodically do things for others and not be concerned about who gets the credit. It's an adventure for the giver as well as for the one who is blessed.

One day my friend and I were walking down a dirt road through the forest. It was quite warm and she commented, "Just listen to the wind high in the trees. I wish a little breeze would blow down here." Suddenly, a cool breeze dipped low and cooled our bodies. It was as if God saw our need and appreciated our awareness of His presence and gave us another reason to praise Him. *Thank you, Lord.*

Leading Others to Christ

The height of adventure for a Christian is to lead another to the Lord. It brings satisfaction to the depth of our souls to take someone's hand and place it in the hand of the Father. We share the love of God as well as their joy as they accept Jesus as Lord.

Our daughter's friend, Kathleen, came to live with us. She'd led a sordid and tumultuous life. She began going to church with us and decided she wanted to be baptized. We all went to the church building one night to witness her new birth. Our daughter's boyfriend, Stan, came along. When Carey brought Kathleen up out of the water, Stan shouted, "Praise God, it's a baby girl!"

It's an incredible blessing when one is born again. God files our birth certificate in the Book of Life with the rest of His children. When Kathleen walked out of the baptistry, she was not only dripping wet with water, but dripping with new possibilities that come with a new commitment to Christ.

What a challenge to Peter and Andrew when Jesus gave them the invitation to come with Him and he would show them how to fish for the souls of men! (See Matthew 4:19). There are positive things to do, souls to save and thresholds to step over when Almighty God calls us to follow Him.

It's an adventure to see how God works in tiny ways as well as huge ones. Sometimes I'm amazed at the little details God works out for me. It's also a thrill to find little jewels of wisdom tucked away in scripture. Adventure promises to *inspire* until we *expire*.

Faithful to the End

My husband, Carey, prepared to leave on his last adventure. A few days before he died, he made a recording and asked for it to be played at his funeral. He encouraged Christians to express themselves in animated praise during worship.

When Bill Bright, head of *Campus Crusade for Christ* was dying, then President George Bush called him on the phone to express concern over his illness. After he hung up, Bill turned to those in the room and said, "That was wonderful for the president to call, but it doesn't compare to the excitement and adventure I'm about to experience. I'm soon to meet the King of kings and the Lord of lords!"

We can look on the Christian life as a battery of tests we take on the way to graduate from this life. "Do you see what this means—all these pioneers who blazed the way, all these veterans cheering us on? It means we'd better get on with it. Strip down, start running—and never quit! No extra spiritual fat, no parasitic sins. Keep your eyes on *Jesus*, who both began and finished this race we're in. Study how he did it. Because he never lost sight of where he was headed" (Hebrews 12:1 MSG). I like to think of loved ones who've gone before us as this crowd in heaven— jumping up and down to cheer us on.

How exciting it is to look up at God's waterfall of blessings and experience them as they come cascading down in thrilling ways. The journey into God's infinite love will mark our last victory as we cross the river into eternity. I'm confident this will be the greatest adventure we'll ever experience.

Lord, give us opportunities to experience the adventure that comes from helping others. And give us the perseverance to hold steady until we take our last breath.

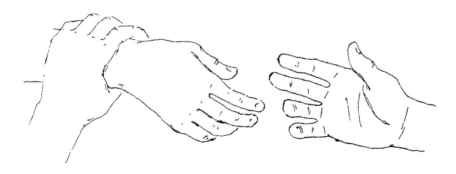

SCRIPTURES TO CONSIDER

1 Corinthians 9:22,23
2 Corinthians 2:14
Ephesians 4:22-24
Hebrews 12:1

QUESTIONS FOR DISCUSSION

1. The greatest adventure I ever had was . . .

2. I feel boredom most often when . . .

3. The way a Christian can put off his old self is by . . .

4. Some things Christians have to deal with and get rid of in order to live a better Christian life is . . .

5. An activity my family did that gave us a feeling of adventure was. . .

6. Spiritual activities that give me a feeling of adventure are.. . .

9

POWER TO OVERCOME

Empowered by the Holy Spirit

Jason was in charge of a group of delinquent teen age boys who went on a three day hiking trip in the mountains. One of the boys was belligerent and uncooperative. Finally, Jason picked up a heavy stone and told the teen he had to carry the rock for the rest of the day. "If you refuse, you won't get anything to eat." The youth grumbled as he grudgingly took the stone. He'd only carried it about half an hour when Jason went to him and said, "Here, let me carry the rock for you."

The young man stammered, "What do you mean?"

"What I'm doing is an example of what Jesus did for me. I rebelled against God, but Jesus took my sins and carried them to the cross. By taking this rock from you, it's a reminder of the loving kindness God has shown me."

Jason could have pulled rank on the young man, but instead, he chose to act as a servant. He became an example of meekness—power under control. The young man was blown away by this graphic act of compassion. As the teen handed the rock back to Jason, he vowed he'd not give his leader any more trouble for the rest of the trip.

This is the kind of example the world longs for. Rather than the forceful and dictatorial power of a tyrant, it reflects the life-changing influence that flows from a servant's heart. It is the confident strength that carries us through, walking in the steps of Jesus. An advertisement from years ago illustrated this beautifully: "Tough, but oh so gentle."

A person lacking gutsy commitment heads for the dugout when he doesn't trust God enough to step up to the plate when he faces the challenges of life. But when we make the decision to go to bat, we can be confident God's Holy Spirit will be there to give us direction and the strength to cover the bases and return home to receive the winner's trophy.

The Power of Self-control

In preparation for Christian camp, several of us volunteered to build wooden platforms for tents. One counselor came from a wealthy family and had never done any manual labor. She repeatedly pounded her fingers with the hammer. We suggested she quit, but she refused. In tears, she switched hands so she wouldn't continue to smash the same fingers. She gritted her teeth and with bulldog determination, she proved she could control a hammer and nails! When we're hurting, I believe God wipes our tears with the tip of His finger and gives us the incentive and courage to keep on going.

Power over self requires the discipline of self-control. Wise King Solomon told us "Controlling your temper is better than being a hero who captures a city" (Proverbs 16:32 CEV). How wise. We commit to becoming strong by breaking bad habits and developing new and better ones.

"For God did not give us a spirit of timidity, but a spirit of power and love and self-control" (2 Timothy 1:7 RSV). Lack of self-control leads a person into sin. I don't know of anyone that doesn't have a problem with this fruit of the Spirit—whether it's in an effort to control our tongue or sticking to a diet. It's reassuring to know that there is no sin we can't resist. "No test or temptation that comes your way is beyond the course of what others have had to face. All you need to remember is that God will never let you down; he'll never let you be pushed past your limit; he'll always be there to help you come through it" (1 Cor. 10:13 MSG).

We experience power when we pull back on the reins of self-control. We gain self-confidence by staying on track. We gallop ahead when we make good choices. But even when we get confused and shout "gee" instead of "haw," we can make an "about face" and try again. We need to recognize the times when wisdom would have us dismount and get on our faces to ask God for the ability to stay on course.

Parental Control

Some parents are overly-protective of their children—not wanting them to fall or fail. Life however, involves risks. Even a small child needs to experience some failure and disappointment. Or else, in later years, when the parents are no longer around to hover over them, difficult problems will seem overwhelming. Parents who protect their children from life's challenges become enablers and their offsprings become helpless. Learning to engage life and difficult times is a step toward maturity.

Parents can't always face situations with the same game plan. Even when a method of disciplining has been successful in dealing with one child, it may not work with the next. There was a time when I had no children and a lot of theories. Then, I had a lot of children and no theories. My floundering to know how to handle a situation often left me befuddled. It's necessary to continue to seek God's wisdom in dealing with each child and each circumstance. I didn't always do that, and as a result, my children and I both suffered consequences.

People have commented on how well my children turned out. I respond by saying, "God had to work hard with them to undo a lot of my mistakes." They grew up well, not because of me, but in spite of me.

It brings comfort to most of us to know we *all* make mistakes and experience failures because of the way we've handled situations. Our divine textbook reminds us we can seek supernatural wisdom to learn to be better parents. "Fathers, don't exasperate your children by coming down hard on them. Take them by the hand and lead them in the way of the Master" (Ephesians 6:4 MSG).

Power Comes from Tackling Big Projects

When my brother's sons came to ask him how to repair a piece of equipment, he'd close one eye and press his lips together. "Did someone make this thing?" They'd shake their heads in confusion, "Well, yes, of course." He'd point his finger at them with a few staccato dots and challenge them, "Then you can find a way to fix it." His sons matured as competent men—able to tackle almost every tough problem that faced them.

In the poem *Invictus,* William Earnest Henley surmised: "I am the master of my fate, the captain of my soul." Henley missed God's point. When we choose to follow God, *He* becomes the master of our fate and the Commander-in-chief of our soul. Thank you, Lord. The weight of responsibility for victorious living was never meant to rest entirely on our shoulders.

The Apostle Paul expressed his inability to control his life in Romans 7, but later he learned where he had to go for his strength. "I can do all this through him who gives me strength" (Philippians 4:13 NIV).

A Silent Way to Exert Power

Power over others can come in the form of leadership and influence. The way we respond to life's demands has the potential of becoming a powerful example to inspire others. The world would much rather see an example of right living than for us to give them a rule book. Wordless, yet loud messages are conveyed by courageous examples. Silent leadership, based on wisdom, sends a loud and clear message to the world.

When I taught in an elementary school, I don't remember mentioning to my principle that I was a Christian, yet on two different occasions, she called me into her office and asked me to pray for her.

My Mom was a woman of few words, but she wielded tremendous influence and left a lasting impression on her eight children. We were amazed at the way she handled poverty, sickness and disappointments. She had a confident faith that God would see us through any obstacle that sprang up along the way.

We were amused and relieved when she laughed at things that would have caused others to become angry or upset. When my brother was a teen, he was working in the yard outside the kitchen window and Mom tossed a glass of water on him. In retaliation, he grabbed the water hose and ran inside and sprayed water on her *and* the kitchen floor. She burst into laughter over my brother's response to her prank. Her joyous spirit spoke volumes to all who knew her.

"Here's another way to put it: You're here to be light, bringing out the God-colors in the world . . .If I make you light-bearers, you don't think I'm going to hide you under a bucket, do you? I'm putting you on a light stand. Now that I've put you there on a hilltop, on a light stand—shine! Keep open house; be generous with your lives. By opening up to others, you'll prompt people to open up with God . . ." (Matthew 5:14-16 MSG).

One may believe his life isn't a strong influence if he's the only Christian in a work-place. But I'm reminded of when I went to Carlsbad Caverns. In the depths of the cave, the guide asked us to stand still. He switched off all the lights. I'd never witnessed pitch blackness. Darkness, like evil, became so intense we could feel it. Our guide struck a match and it appeared far brighter than seemed possible. Our influence is like that. It shines its brightest in dark places—so whether we are a candle or a beacon, we have an opportunity to light the way for those following us.

We Feel Power When We're Creative

When we're creative, it gives us satisfaction that floods our well-being. We feel the same when we successfully complete a project or find a solution to a nagging problem. The feeling of power is enhanced when we help others in the process. Tiny flickers of power are reflected in things as simple as making a lovely floral arrangement or completing a crossword puzzle.

On the other hand, we're frustrated and lose the feeling of power when we're unable to accomplish a seemingly simple task. I experience this when I can't find a way keep the squirrels from eating all the seed in my bird feeder. (I hate to admit squirrels are better at problem-solving than I am.)

Power over circumstances is evident when we complete a task that we had no idea we could complete. Our faith is enhanced and builds a framework until we're confident there's nothing impossible with God. Our Lord shows His delight by using unlikely people to perform supernatural feats. This was evident in a tiny little woman, Mother Teresa, who came from an obscure country, but whose life impacted the world.

How refreshing that God also left room for His children to en-hance worship in creative and powerful ways. King David exhibited delightful exuberance when he danced before the Lord. I believe he sensed God's approval when he expressed his enthusiasm with uninhibited praise.

On the other hand, tradition can become so ingrained in worship that "dyed-in-the-wool church-goers" get upset if traditions are changed. Under the guise of making sure everything is "decent and in order," they enforce rigid rules until the service reeks with moldy staleness. Truth shouldn't be a leash, but a guide. We're not to be tethered to traditions but rather linked to God. Delightful worship sparkles with creativity and spontaneity.

A minister visited a church that was boring and appeared to be dying. He dreaded spending the day there. The song leader led the songs—dragging them with no sign of joy or life. The prayers were memorized phrases. One member prayed for "the sick of this congregation." The visiting minister said he had only been there twenty minutes and he was already sick of that congregation. He reported that people who just sit in pews to crank out a form of religion may be considered "putrid" in God's sight. What a blessing it would be if the fresh winds of the Spirit would blow through as a wake-up call for the members to become exuberant and filled with joy.

The Source of Power and the Abundant Life

Power for an effective and abundant life comes from our Father, His Son Jesus and the resources available through His Holy Spirit. Our Almighty Father is able to shake mountains, throw lightning bolts across the sky, tip the waters of the oceans and flood the earth with a tsunami. What a mighty God we serve!

The power of God's love was given to us as Jesus "strung the wire" from heaven to earth in order to reach out to mankind. Picture the transmitting wire being held up by the crossbar on Jesus' cross. It would be like a telephone pole with wire strung across the top. The wire coming from God could represent the blessings Jesus brings to us from heaven. The returning wire would be our prayers, also strung over the horizontal bar of the cross, traveling from man back to God. This cross, of course, is a symbol of Jesus' sacrificial death. What a blessed reassurance that God's power is available through this divine arrangement.

The Holy Spirit is the transformer for this transference of power.

The power that comes from God is reduced so that it will not overwhelm or short-circuit our mental capacity. As long as we're plugged into our relationship to the Father, we have open access to His unlimited power. The Spirit transforms man's weak and wobbly prayers, and then amplifies them until we appear in the throne room as powerful intercessors. For us, the cross is the melding point of God's love and man's faith. Devoted lives connected to God assure us these wires will continue to link us to our Heavenly Father and never fall to the ground to cause us to lose this supernatural resource.

Father, may we keep prayers flowing upward over the "wire" strung over the cross to You. We wait in anticipation for blessings to flow down from Your throne room by the way of the cross, completing this supernatural cycle.

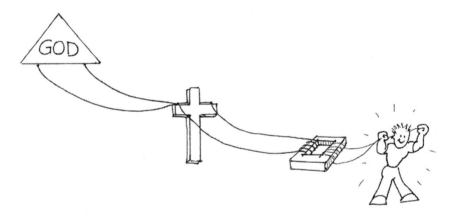

SCRIPTURES TO CONSIDER

Romans 5:6–11
Ephesians 2:5–10
Acts 5:30–31
1 Corinthians 2:9

QUESTIONS FOR DISCUSSION

1. I can meet my need for power over *self* by. . .

2. I meet my need for power over *others* through. . .

3. I meet my need for power over *things* by. . .

4. I feel God's power in my life the most when. . .

5. What part do works play in living the Christian life? . . .

6. What does it mean to you when you call Jesus "Lord"?

10

THE NEED TO SUCCEED

Go for the gold

Success is the meat and potatoes of our needs. Even a two-year old wants to feel competent by declaring, "I do it myself."

The Apostle Paul must have sighed wondrous relief when he wrote, "I have fought the fight, I have finished the course, I have kept the faith—Now there is in store for me the crown of righteousness, which the Lord, the righteous Judge, will award to me on that day—and not only to me, but also to all who have longed for his appearing" (2 Timothy 4:7 NIV).

Though Paul initially persecuted the followers of Jesus, he made a complete turnaround when he surrendered his life to Jesus. He prepared for "graduation" by passing lifelong tests under the tutorage of the Master Teacher. He knew that successful living involved God-ordained rules and kept his commitment to trust in God, fully confident he'd be rewarded.

In a similar fashion, at the end, Jesus triumphantly cried out, "It is finished!" God looks forward to His children finishing well. As the President of "Hard Knocks University," He is pleased to honor us as we graduate *Suma Cum Laude*. That image causes me to catch my breath in wonder and fall to my knees in humble gratitude.

God Gives Us the Ability to Succeed

God-aspiring faith is the ladder that allows us to climb closer to Him. Each rung gives us the warm satisfaction of knowing we're drawing near the top to bask in the light of His presence. Bits of success inject strength and the motivation so we can keep climbing higher and gives us the ability to tackle more difficult challenges along the way.

Giving up is not an option. We understand that mountain-top experiences may only come after we've climbed out of the valleys of defeat—after we've traversed a wilderness of trials. Christianity does not allow us to sit around and mope, but gives us a life that continues to move forward with hope.

King David wasn't hesitant to ask God for success. He asked the Lord to help them, save them and give them success. (See Psalms 118:25). Ordinary people working with an extraordinary God can climb to unimaginable heights. "God can do anything, you know— far more than you could ever imagine or guess or request in your wildest dreams! He does it not by pushing us around but by working within us, his Spirit deeply and gently within us" (Ephesians 3:20 MSG). How blessed we are.

God's Way May Be Different

God's path may not be the route we'd choose. We're bound to encounter detours, but there are no dead-end streets. The rails to success consist of parallel tracks of honesty and integrity. Honesty keeps us transparent and integrity keeps us trustworthy.

Some of Satan's most vicious attacks involve his attempts to convince us we're simply not capable of living a successful life. Our Father challenges us. Rather than considering that we face tasks we *can't* do, moving forward may be a matter of what we *can do* with His strength. It's natural for us to measure our success by what others have done.

My dad reminded me that my two older sisters were valedictorians in high school. (I was not.) I felt inadequate and became discouraged, but I came to know with certainty that while rock bottom may be as far down as we can go, there's no limit as to how high we can soar. With dogged determination, I made the president's honor roll in graduate school.

Success may depend on how tenacious we are in developing a strong relationship with God. Our Father leads us to a place that is far more than survival mentality. According to the parable of the talents, God expects us to be successful with whatever gifts and talents He's entrusted to us. Some believe these blessings are conditional—"use it or lose it." However, "God's gifts and God's call are under full warranty—never canceled, never rescinded" (Romans 11:29 MSG).

Even when we've buried our talents until they are dormant and seem no longer useful, they can be resurrected at any time and developed. Many outstanding people, such as Grandma Moses, didn't dig their talents out until they were what the world considered "old." I didn't start writing until I was about 75 years old. There's never a time to throw up our hands and declare "You can't teach an old dog new tricks."

It's nothing short of an insult to God when we fail to develop the talents He's blessed us with. It's a sad commentary for us to be mediocre when we could be outstanding.

Mediocre is living between the best of the worst and the worst of the best.

As a trained athlete, we're to "go for the gold. "Anyone, then, who knows the good they ought to do and doesn't do it, sins" (James 4:17 NIV). Paul teaches emphatically in Romans 8 that God has given us the Holy Spirit so we can be successful—to be "more than conquerors." In God's hands, nothing is ordinary.

Success Is Relative

Thank goodness success doesn't mean we must be a world champion or even the winner in a local contest. We participate in an element of success when we're a part of a cheering section and put on our boots and spur others on. We're able to experience some of their exuberance.

Growth and progress should be counted as success. We need to be thankful for how far we've come rather than bemoan how far we need to go. A teacher can give a child the feeling of satisfaction when she tells him, "Johnny, that's the best picture you've ever drawn." It may still be one of the poorest pictures in the classroom, but if it's the best the child can do, that's progress. He deserves recognition. A person recovering from a crippling accident celebrates progress when he takes his first step in physical therapy. Success shouts "yes," as we overcome each roadblock standing between us and our goal.

Our son played football in high school. He was one of the smallest on the team and not necessarily a great player, but at the awards banquet at the end of the year, the coach gave him a trophy: "The Fighting Heart Award," because Rick worked hard and did his best.

Our records here on earth may be no match for a Bill Bright or a Billy Graham, but if we're committed to God, He's pleased with our efforts. We wait in joyful anticipation to hear Him say, "Well done, good and faithful servant."

Keep a Record of Successes

It is unfortunate that there are those who keep score of failures rather than successes. Each of us *will* make mistakes and fall short of our expectations. My brother told Mom he was thinking of resigning as editor of the school annual because some had criticized his work. Our mother wisely challenged him, "If you don't want to be criticized, then don't ever do *anything.*"

There's an old adage, "fall down seven times, stand up eight." Those who focus on mistakes don't get up the first time, much less the eighth. Pessimists discount compliments when others point to their accomplishments by responding, "Yeah, but. . ." If one has adopted a failure mentality, they can't fathom the possibility of succeeding. When Satan accuses him of being incompetent, he tends to agree and say "Yeah, you're right." If that happens, the deceiver has won another battle.

After I completed my first book, I prayed. "Father if this book is not successful, I pray I'll focus on the things I learned in the process of writing, rather than considering my time and efforts a waste."

I want to continue to release the things I do to God, to let it be *His* decision as to what He'll do with my work. Failure can be a learning experience as long as we seek what God wants to teach us in the process.

When others put us down or imply we're a failure, we tend to rehearse their comments and even begin to look for evidence that will confirm their negative opinions. Suppose a wife wears a new dress and nine people tell her it looks great. Then her husband responds, "That thing looks weird." She may never wear that article of clothing again. It's sad that one negative response can overrule every positive comment.

Perfectionists are never completely satisfied with the way any job is completed. A friend who has a tendency toward perfectionism has a sign above her desk, "Perfect is the enemy of good." She is a writer and knows her work will never be finished if she spends too much time "perfecting" it. In graduate school, I minored in art, and the head of the art department told me, "Louise, you never know when to quit."

Parents must be careful to never short-circuit their children's potential by demanding perfect performance. Bite your lip if you must and close your eyes if it helps, but commend them when they try.

Count Bits of Success

We need evidence of daily success. It's a long hard day and night if we fail to feel we've succeeded in some way. Success shouldn't be a source of pride, but it can give us a sense of well-being to know our efforts have not been in vain.

God says, "You are a chosen people, a royal priesthood, a holy nation, God's special possession, that you may declare the praises of him who called you out of darkness into his wonderful light" (1 Peter 2:9 NIV). It's doubtful we'll ever be given a more powerful endorsement.

Even on days when it seems we've accomplished only a "piddling" amount, we can count it as success if we've maintained a good attitude. Rather than kick ourselves for not doing more or doing a better job, we can praise God that He's preparing us for a greater tomorrow. He may allow our plans to be scrapped to teach us patience or perseverance. We are to be grateful for small things in preparation for celebrating larger accomplishments.

Our MDR

Just as we have a MDR (Minimum Daily Requirement) for vitamins, we need to have a MDR for success. We should keep a record of things we've done well or ways we've helped others, whether it's in our work, at home or in our hobbies. Our greatest successes always include others.

In younger years, I played the piano when I was disappointed or had failed at something. The music not only comforted me, but confirmed there was something I could do reasonably well.

Our previous accomplishments reaffirm we can do a good job at something. It lifts our spirits. We use talents to edify God and help others, as well as fortifying us against discouragement.

Failure

Failure gouges holes in our reservoir, draining away a good self-image. Feelings of failure come from situations as significant as being fired from a job to simply burning the toast in the morning. My husband used to tell others I worshipped him, because I gave him burnt offerings almost every day.

One year at Christmas, we gave our daughter miniature kitchen appliances. The set included a tiny toaster with plastic slices of bread. My brother-in-law was visiting, and he observed our four year old son, Rick, getting a knife from the drawer. He asked, "What are you doing?" Rick answered matter-of-factly, "Well, we need a knife to scrape the toast." I cringed, because I'd taught him well!

Failures may dampen our spirits as surely as if it'd been written across a person's forehead. One look in a mirror confirms it. "Yep, that's me—a failure." Such an attitude leads one to this conclusion because he's kept score of what he's done wrong rather than what he's done right.

When we stoop to pointing out one of our family member's failures, it can have a devastating effect. Such repeated recordings need to be deleted. Rather than criticizing, we'd do well to offer them a helping hand—and do that without making them feel inadequate.

We must never allow failure to drag us down in despondency. Failure can be flipped to a positive when we realize that God's strength and wisdom are able to bring us into *His* definition of success. Don't ignore the beautiful fact that God is pointing to the stairway that rises to an overcoming walk that He has planned for us.

Soon, for all of us, the game of life will end. The whistle will blow and our final score will be recorded in the Book of Life. We're promised that those who've played by the rules will be called to walk on streets of gold. Now that's success!

Lord, teach us how to accomplish what <u>You</u> consider to be success in our lives. Show us how to respond to failure with the realization that You're still at work on our worst days. Remind us to express our praise because Your miraculous power is able to resurrect beauty from ashes.

SCRIPTURES TO CONSIDER

Matthew 25:14–30
Romans 8:31–39
Ephesians 6:5–8
1 John 5:3–5

QUESTIONS FOR DISCUSSION

1. Some activities I feel success in are . . .

2. The "thing" I am best in is . . .

3. I would really like to become good in . . .

4. Do I keep score of my failures more than successes? Explain.

5. Some of the ways I can encourage those I'm around to feel success is by . . .

6. What does it mean when scripture tells us tht we were once in darkness, but now are in the light? . . .

SECTION III
THINGS GET IN THE WAY

11

PEOPLE AND CIRCUMSTANCES PULL THE PLUG

Help! I'm draining dry

A teacher stood in front of her classroom with a large white sheet of paper with a small smudge in the center of it. She asked: "Tell me what you see." Her students pointed to the spot they believed marred the paper. Only one student noted, "Since the paper is so much larger than the little dark spot, I noticed the paper." We too must remember to look at the whole picture, not just point out the flaws we notice.

It's sad to find we live in an imperfect world where insensitive people hurt others by puncturing their egos. We may even be perceptive enough to brace ourselves when a negative person comes on the scene, because we know from experience how often they tend to punch holes in our buckets.

Painful emotional cracks can damage our egos because we continue to leak good feelings. Some may not be aware they've hurt us—so we may need to pray as Jesus did, "Father, forgive them, for they do not know what they are doing" (Luke 23:34 NIV). Still others don't have a clue, don't care, how cutting words continue to hurt. "Some people like to make cutting remarks, but the words of the wise soothe and heal" (Proverbs 12:18 TLB). This should be a reminder to keep a healing balm of positive scriptures near to apply as needed.

Not All Is Right With the World

While visiting my mother-in-law, I stood at the kitchen sink doing dishes. My sister-in-law sat at the breakfast table and sarcastically remarked to my husband, "I've heard your wife has some weird religious beliefs." I carefully dried my hands and laid my hand on her shoulder. "Jean★, watch my life. If that doesn't give you a clear picture as to what I believe, it makes no difference what others tell you." I could have uttered "*touché,*" but quietly went back to washing dishes while she glared at me.

Her remark stung a bit, but considering it was just a small jab, I chinked that hole by reaffirming that God was okay with my relationship with Him. I remembered that irritating people tend to stretch our faith, but God uses these same people as a resource to build our character.

Grouchy people drain us gradually, but they still cause our tanks to leak. In Charles Shultz's famous comic strip *Peanuts*, Lucy told Charley Brown, "I was just born with crabby genes." An old expression described that type of person as one weaned on a lemon and soured on life.

Darts at Ten Paces

Masochistic people make a game of draining reservoirs because that's their nature. For example, a husband may come home from work at six o'clock. There's no food prepared and the house is a mess. He selects a dart and targets his wife. "Why isn't supper ready? Have you been stretched out on the couch watching those stupid soap operas all afternoon?"

He doesn't understand that it's been a difficult day for his wife and her reservoir is already low. She whips a dart from the tip of her tongue and slings it back. "I've worked all day taking care of sick kids and mopping up messes when they threw up. Not only that, I've washed the dirty clothes you dropped on the floor wherever you pleased. All you do is sit around in a plush office and order people around all day."

Her husband now reaches for a larger dart and aims carefully. "I'm on the job slaving to make a living for you and the kids and then come home to a filthy house and a nagging wife."

She follows with her *coup de grace*, "You call THIS living?" So the fight is on. The battle may last for thirty minutes or thirty years. Neither is compassionate enough to look at the conflict from the other's viewpoint. Sadly, no one wins and bloody darts remain strewn across the battlefield.

Stubbornness has become the cholesterol that has hardened their attitudes.

Secondary Battles

In a cartoon series, a wife sitting at the breakfast table shakes her finger in her husband's face, airing her complaints. He doesn't have time to retaliate, so he bites his lip and leaves for work. At the office, he vents his frustration on one of his employees. The employee doesn't dare fight back because he'd likely lose his job, so he grits his teeth and heads back to his desk.

But when the employee gets home, he yells at his son for playing the drums so loud. The child isn't permitted to talk back to his dad, so he kicks the dog. The dog runs outside and the boss's wife, who started the whole scenario, comes walking down the street, and the dog runs out and bites her. This is a classic example of "what goes around comes around."

Cast your bread upon the waters and it will come back—buttered or burnt.

We complain about people who lose their temper, but unfortunately, it's never lost—only tucked away to be whipped out in a split second in another explosion. And the blasts are seldom confined to one area. They have a "shotgun" effect and children get wounded in the cross-fire.

Cold Shoulder at a Closer Range

Another game is depicted. Coming home in the evening, a husband finds the newspaper scattered and his wife can't remember where she put the mail. He clenches his teeth as evidence that anger is grinding on his nerves and rising to the surface, but he says nothing. He'll simply not take out the trash or help set the table. The wife holds her tongue and doesn't gripe at him for not helping, but she's not about to bring him a bowl of ice cream after supper.

No darts have been thrown—but both react, giving the other the strong, silent treatment. Her attitude expresses, *if that guy's not doing anything for me, I'm sure not doing anything for him.* After a few cycles, hearts and shoulders grow cold and indifferent. The message of rejection cuts gashes in their emotional reservoirs. Though it's largely internal "bleeding," the relationship becomes dangerously anemic. We all find it difficult to tend to other's needs when we're nursing our own wounds.

Don't Get Even

When I was a little girl, I got mad at my older sister and followed her around and called her names. Eventually she turned and said, "I am so glad you're my little sister. I don't know what I'd do without you." I'll never forget that. It stopped me cold in my four-year-old tracks when she broke the cycle by being kind when I'd called her ugly names.

If someone purposely pushes us, our first response is to shove them back. Emotionally, when someone pierces our ego with a psychological dart, we're tempted to hurl a dart back— harder. Instead, we could pretend to pull the dart out with a dramatic gesture and reply, "Ouch, that hurt! Do you have a band-aid to patch the hole?" Hopefully, they'll get the point.

When people choose to fill themselves with themselves, it displeases God. "My people have committed two sins: They have forsaken me, the spring of living water, and have dug their own cisterns, broken cisterns that cannot hold water" (Jeremiah 2:13 NIV).

No matter how good one is at winning an argument, putting others down or getting the last word, it never takes care of their own needs. Such behavior may give them a small boost and make them feel smug or superior for a brief moment, but just as helium loses its lift, one-upmanship loses its ability to keep one floating on a cloud.

Empty Containers Represent Emotional Thirst

Many who have been deeply hurt in childhood develop an insatiable thirst. It's understandable when they continue to walk around with a low reservoir—one that's difficult to fill. Researchers tell us that the younger a child is when he's emotionally wounded, the more difficult it is to get over that hurt. The person often needs professional help in order to pick up the pieces and put his life together so it "holds water" again.

My sister-in-law adopted a three-year-old boy who came from a horrible background. Scars on his body indicated he'd been burned with cigarettes. He was psychologically damaged and struggled with problems for the rest of his life. He even added to his problems with self-inflicted wounds as an evidence of self-hatred. This is an example of the sins of forefathers being passed from one generation to the next.

For some, regardless of what is said or done, they discount words that were meant as encouragement. It's obvious that their psychological tanks leak. The search is on to find how to mend cracks and patch holes.

We know Jesus is the only "super glue" guaranteed to hold it all together.

People and Things Fill the Reservoir

We can be thankful there's a better way to live! If we're persistent, we'll discover things that fill emotional tanks. I think Snicker Bars are scrumptious. My husband often bought a bag of the miniature ones and hid them. When I did something that pleased him, he'd get a Snicker Bar from his secret stash and toss it to me. I wouldn't just snicker, I'd laugh right out loud. It satisfied my sweet tooth, but it also filled my love tank.

We're not only commanded to supply spiritual needs, but we're also to take care of physical and emotional emptiness. There's a great game we might call "buckets at two paces." We play it as we recognize and meet another person's needs. "And if anyone gives even a cup of cold water to one of these little ones who is my disciple, truly I tell you, that person will certainly not lose their reward"(Matthew 10:42 NIV).

Jesus gave a clearer picture : "I was hungry and you fed me, I was thirsty and you gave me a drink, I was homeless and you gave me a room, I was shivering and you gave me clothes, I was sick and you stopped to visit, I was in prison and you came to visit me'"(Matthew 25:35-36 MSG.). Let the Living Water flow!

Father, fill my cup until it overflows into the lives of those surrounding me. Teach me how to look at the overall picture, to refuse to be critical or put others down. Give me words of encouragement that flow from my lips, to water those whose reservoirs are running low.

SCRIPTURES TO CONSIDER

Jeremiah 2:13
Matthew 10:420
Matthew 25:35-36
Romans 7:15-25
Romans 12:13

QUESTIONS FOR DISCUSSION

1. <u>Someone</u> causes me to feel empty and drained when they
   . . .

2. <u>Something</u> that happened that caused me to feel drained was
   when . . .

3. People fill my reservoir when they . . .

4. Someone gave me a cold shoulder when they . . .

5. Things went wrong and I had to be patient when . . .

6. The way I can keep others from controlling my emotions is
   by . . .

12

PERSONALITY POISONS

I didn't see the skull and cross-bones on the label

There's laundry lists of things that poison the personality. Some are so common they seem to sit around the house like dirty clothes in a laundry basket. We take into account that our approach to life typically comes from two distinct mind-sets—pessimism or optimism. Pessimism is covered with stubborn stains of hopelessness, while optimism is washed in hope.

Pessimism and Negativism

Pessimism is a foundation upon which negativism is built. The character "Puddleglum" in C.S. Lewis' *Chronicles of Narnia* was so negative, he complained about everything that was wrong in life and discounted anything positive. If a situation turned sour, he'd grumble, "I just *knew* it wasn't going to work." He went through life with his eyes looking at the trash on the ground, never bothering to look up and be grateful for God's blessings.

Sadly, negativism is contagious. It's like coughing without covering our mouth, spreading germs until everyone around is as sick as we are. We contaminate the atmosphere with our complaints and infect others with a grumpy virus. Pessimism and gloom reek with sickening unpleasantness.

We have opportunities to reverse negativity through God's blessed promise that He can renew our minds. God knew the tendency of some to be negative and critical, so he prompted us all to: "Take captive every thought to make it obedient to Christ" (2 Corinthians 10:5 NIV).

Negative People Discourage Us

Dry winds of discouragement may create a veritable dust bowl of drought in our spirits. In desperation, we may look in the wrong places to fill the emptiness. Without discernment, we could trudge toward a mirage, only to fall in exhaustion as we watch our hope evaporate before our eyes. Our last bit of strength has been used in search of something to fill this insatiable thirst.

What a shame to walk away from the Holy Spirit's Living Water to follow the crowd. Even worse is if we stoop to that of a con artist, draining others in an attempt to meet our own selfish needs.

There are negative "know-it-alls" who rail against everyone by disagreeing with them. These individuals should be reminded that God doesn't give anyone a license to put others down. It's useless to argue with these people because they display an attitude, "My mind's made up—don't confuse me with the facts."

Our minds are like parachutes—no good unless open. Like the clanging cymbals described in First Corinthians 13, the less substance in an argument, the noisier some people become. My husband thought the reason some preachers shouted was because their points were too weak to stand on their own.

Prejudices and Old Wives Tales

People are often prejudiced without logical reasoning. I caught my father gently pulling on my baby's ears. A bit concerned, I asked, "What are you doing?"

Dad looked a little sheepish, but replied, "When their ears stick close to their head, it's a sign they're stingy." (He undoubtedly thought himself generous, because his own ears flopped outside his head.)

The range of beliefs and prejudices is wide. They discriminate against those with different lengths of hair, different accents, or those who live on the "wrong side of the tracks." When we lived in the Dallas area, a deacon at church kicked his son out of their home because he wouldn't cut his hair. He later confessed, "The length of his hair was not worth losing a son."

If we're courageous enough, we'll ask our family to give us some kind of a signal to let us know when we show up with a stinky attitude toward others. Ask them to pull on their earlobe or close their eyes as a reminder for us to get serious about maintaining an upbeat attitude.

Believers with God-like characteristics are challenged to set an example for others by breaking down walls of prejudice. When we do, we become more like God. He is not prejudiced. "Then Peter opened his mouth, and said, of a truth I perceive that God is no respecter of persons" (Acts 10:34 NIV).

Salty Waters of Selfishness

Salt water could represent selfishness—that which dries up good character traits. People with selfish personalities are like the Dead Sea—always taking or receiving, but not allowing Living Water to flow through to others. As a consequence, their own lives are never hydrated because they've failed to quench the thirst of those who follow them. Pessimism hardens around their feet until they're stuck in doom and gloom.

Just as water from the ocean dehydrates the human body, the psychological immune system wilts when a person centers on himself. Our healthy egos shrivel when another dumps criticism on us. Critical remarks usually make us feel dumb or inadequate. Fortunately, we can blossom again when people water us with affirmations.

Get Rid of Your Garbage

If we refuse to identify and deal with underlying psychological defects in our lives, they become like old garbage. The longer we let this trash set around, the smellier it becomes. After a time, we can use a biblical implication, "Yea, verily it stinketh!" It's high time to find the rotting potatoes in our attitudes and get rid of them. We must trust God to sanitize our bad thoughts, words and actions.

Our failures tempt us to use blobs of rationalization to patch weak character traits. There's a fine line between rationalizing and releasing a situation to God. We're not to brush off failure when we don't achieve the goals we've set. Yet, we trust God's ability to work out what best for us, regardless of where we are or what has happened.

We determine to choose to walk through doors the Lord opens and refrain from becoming pessimistic when doors fail to open as we'd hoped.

One night I had a dream: I opened the door and found my neighbor had put her garbage on my front porch. I struggled with a decision as to what to do with it—whether to take it back next door or simply put it with my trash. Not wanting to cause a problem, I picked it up and included it with my own garbage.

The next morning it shocked me when I realized the dream was a classic example of how I live my life. All too often, I allow people to dump their garbage on me and then I fail to hold them responsible to work on solving at least a portion of their own struggles.

God's grace helps us walk away from negative trends. His Word will fill us with clean thoughts to make our lives rich and full. He wants to keep chiseling off rough edges and polishing us until we begin to look and act more like Jesus.

Pretence Isn't Truthful

At a retreat, a man told his life's story. With a broad grin plastered across his face, he said. "My mom died when I was six, but that was cool, because I got to go live with my grandmother." Incredulous disbelief swept over me, gathering anger on the way to the surface. I squirmed in my chair for a moment before I rose to confront him.

"Don't tell me it was cool for your mother to die. You never really got to know her and experience a mother's love. God did make provisions for you, but it was tragic your mom had to leave you at the tender age of six."

A mind-set can consist of an attitude: "If I can't get what I want, then I'll pretend I got exactly what I wanted." But this resolution is dishonest. This is not the same as the Apostle Paul's response when he said, "I know what it is to be in need, and I know what it is to have plenty. I have learned the secret of being content in any and every situation, whether well-fed or hungry, whether living in plenty or in want" (Philippians 4:12 NIV). He was wise when he adapted to situations so he wasn't stuck in his infamous past.

When heartfelt longings are masked, however, a person may pretend everything is "hunky dory," even though he's devastated. This isn't godly acceptance but an attitude of: "I'll pretend I don't care, rather than admit how agonizing the pain is that is crushing my heart."

Careful! Stuffed emotional pain has a way of surfacing and causing problems that show up in different ways. This includes depression.

Modern Day Scapegoat

In the Old Testament, the sins of the people were laid on what they called a scapegoat. The people figuratively placed their sins on an unblemished goat and it was led into the wilderness, never to allow it to return. It was an attempt to distance themselves from bad things they'd done and said.

Since no one wants to carry heavy buckets of guilt, we too look for a place to dump loads of shame and guilt. Faced with this dilemma, some create their own modern-day scapegoat. But it carries a different meaning from the original concept. Now, we use the term "scapegoat" to explain how an individual slithers out of responsibility. They may even dust their hands and say, "What I've done is not really my fault." It's sad when we use wives or husbands, children, the weather, the church or our government as a form of a scapegoat.

I'm grateful that God gives us the answer: "Summing it all up, friends, I'd say you'll do best by filling your minds and meditating on things true, noble, reputable, things to praise, not things to curse . . . Do that and God, who makes everything work together, will work you into His most excellent harmonies" (Philippians 4:9 MSG).

Check Me Out

Our motives are not always evident. I need to constantly ask God. "Investigate my life, O God, find out everything about me; Cross-examine and test me, get a clear picture of what I'm about, see for yourself whether I've done anything wrong—then guide me on the road to eternal life!" (Psalms 139:24 MSG).

The world shouts for us to conform, while God whispers for us to be transformed. Scripture tells us "We have the mind of Christ" (1 Corinthians 2:16 NIV). In this way, we guard our thoughts and keep our eyes on the road we've been assigned to travel.

Keep on Keeping on

"So let us run the race that is before us and never give up. We should remove anything from our lives that would get in our way and the sin that so easily holds us back. Let us look only to Jesus, the one who began our faith and makes it perfect" (Hebrews 12:1-2 NCV).

What a blessing to realize our compassionate Father takes care of *all* our needs. He sent the Lamb of God, Jesus Christ, as our redeemer. (This Lamb, unlike the scapegoat, was perfect inside, not just on the outside.)

All our past, present and future sins were placed on Him and put to death on that cross. The weight of shame and guilt was completely removed from our shoulders. He isn't the typical scapegoat that we place our sins on to get them out of our sight, but a sacrificial lamb who takes on our sins for them to die with Him. They are completely done away with. *Thank you, Lord.*

How sad if we don't accept Jesus' death on the cross as the blessed provision He planned for us. It was there He allowed our sins and flawed thinking to be the nails in His hands and feet. He received the punishment we deserved—not as a scapegoat, but as the Lamb of God—offered so the darkest of sins could be forever erased from our records.

The blood dripping from Jesus' wounds drained the life from His body, but became the blood transfusion we needed for us to live a triumphant life. His crown of thorns purchased a crown of righteousness for us that signifies that we have been redeemed as a child of the King.

Lord, keep us from being disgruntled and maintaining a sour attitude about life. Teach me how to get rid of personality poisons and revive a grateful heart that offers You praise rather than complaints.

SCRIPTURES TO CONSIDER

2 Corinthians 10:4-5
Acts 10:34-35
Philippians 4:11-12
Psalms 139:23-24
Hebrews 12:1-2

QUESTIONS FOR DISCUSSION

1. Do you consider yourself to be a pessimist or an optimist? Explain your answer.

2. How does someone who is negative make you feel?

3. Do you have a control issue and try to "fix" everything or feel you need to always tell people what to do? Explain

4. Are you now or have you ever been prejudiced? Explain

5. Tell about someone you know who is selfish or always talking about themselves.

6. Is there anything or anyone you blame for how things turned out in your life?

13

REPRESS, SUPPRESS
OR CONFESS

There's no problem too small for me to run away from

Occasionally we see people in their thirties and forties regress in dress, speech and conduct—characteristic of much younger people. Some revert to using teenage jargon. We shake our heads and smile at how ridiculous they act, yet it is a sad commentary when a person isn't willing to adapt to the stage of life he's currently going through. The apostle Paul cautions us. "When I was a child, I talked like a child. When I became a man, I put childish ways behind me" (1 Corinthians 13:11 NIV).

Going Back to Former Ways and Habits

Regression may be an outward expression of an inner desire. "I don't want to grow up or get old." It's a Peter Pan reaction. A forty-five year old woman bemoaned her current status, "I just want to go back to high school when I was a happy cheer leader."

In a seminar, the leader asked a participant to turn loose of one chair and walk to another as a symbolic way of leaving her past and going toward the future. This older woman spoke in a strange, wee voice. "I can't, I'm too wittle."

When I was in the first grade, little Ann wailed as she went up to the teacher's desk and pointed to a hole that had been chewed in her sleeve. "Look at what Dale just did."

The teacher's mouth dropped open and she turned to the six year old sitting next to Ann. "Dale, I asked you not to suck your thumb in class, but chewing on Ann's dress is worse."

A Few Examples of Regression:

- A small child who has been toilet trained begins to have "accidents" after a new baby is born.
- A mental patient lies on the floor and curls up in a fetal position—similar to that of a baby in the womb.
- A thirty or forty-year old has a temper tantrum and throws things, kicks and yells. (This is especially scary, because their childish ways may also include hitting people.)
- An older man presents himself as a dashing young knight in shining armor in an attempt to charm every good-looking woman he sees.
- A woman reverts to giddy teenage flirtation with men of all ages.

Pushing a Memory Out of Mind

When a person buries an incident so deep in his mind he doesn't remember it, we call it *repression*--pushing an unpleasant memory into the subconscious. This is not what the Apostle Paul meant when he said, "Forgetting what is behind and straining toward what is ahead . . ." (Philippians 3:13 NIV). His counsel was to live in the present and look forward to the future, rather than remaining stuck in the past.

We "bog down" when we refuse to deal with situations we face in life. We have a tendency to want to block things from our mind, but it does not alter the consequences emotionally, physically or spiritually. For example, after I had a blood test, I received a note from the doctor. "Your tests reveal some disturbing possibilities. Come back to my office for further testing." I glanced at the note and stuck it in a drawer. "Out of sight, out of mind," I totally forgot about it.

After a week, the doctor's office called. "Why haven't you returned for an additional work-up?" Perhaps I had an underlying fear of a bad report. I apologized and went in for more in-depth testing. The results showed there were no troubling concerns. However, if I'd continued to repress the memory and something had been wrong, the problem would have probably gotten worse.

We may unconsciously block things from our minds that have been painful or traumatic. These displaced files lie somewhere in our subconscious and influence our thoughts and actions. When we're unaware of a problem because we've buried it, it may haunt us with "free-floating" anxiety, a nagging apprehension, and we may not know the source.

This could produce an uneasy feeling of: "I don't know what it is, but I just don't feel right, like something is wrong." The memory may surface years later through flashbacks. These flashbacks may be God's reminder that it's time to deal with the problem, to be set free, in order for us to get on with life.

Facing Our Fears

My husband had a counselee who had an unreasonable fear of feathers and panicked at the sight of a bird or chicken. She trembled when a woman with a feather on her hat came in the room. Even after detailed probing, she couldn't remember what might be defined as the root of the phobia.

Since this was a source of concern and embarrassment to her, Carey had her come in for a series of sessions in which he reconditioned her perception of feathers and birds. First, he put a feather on the window sill. When it ceased to bother her, he laid it on the corner of his desk. Finally, he held the feather in his hand. His client never wanted to hold the feather, but success was realized when she was able to be around feathers, even birds, without panicking.

Some have different ways of dealing with their problems. A deacon at church had the opposite reaction because he had too little fear of feathers. I sat behind him and his wife in church. She'd worn a hat that had a long pheasant feather on it. Being a curious woman, she turned around to look at every new arrival coming into the assembly. Every time she looked back, her feather swatted her husband in the face. After the fifth time, he reached up and snapped the feather in two, allowing it to dangle back and forth. Worshipful reverence and awe flew out the window and the preacher might as well have dismissed his audience.

My Own Fear

Most of my life, I had an inordinate fear of snakes and referred to them as "an instrument of the devil." Even a picture of a snake sent shivers down my spine. After I was grown, I remembered a time when I was a small child, my older brother chased me through the house with a live snake yelling, "I'm going to put this down your back." I screamed in terror as I ran past my mother. She acted as my hero, stepping in front of him to block his way and ordered, "Oh no, you don't. You get that thing out of the house and don't you ever scare your little sister like that again!"

After identifying the source of my fear, I could actually kill snakes that got in the dove cage or were crawling around on the porch outside my door. To a degree, I overcame that paralyzing fear.

This helped since we lived at a farm and had a variety of snakes to deal with—some of which were poisonous. One day when I was gathering eggs, I found a snake curled in a nest eating the eggs. I dashed back into the house and got a pistol to shoot the ugly thing.

My family had the reputation of being expert marksmen, but I couldn't hit "dooly-squat" with a gun. My first bullet hit an egg which splattered. The snake moved slightly. I kept shooting until I almost destroyed the end of the chicken house. Eventually, I killed the snake, but refused to get near enough to remove that dead thing from the nest. From that point on, I was quite cautious when I gathered eggs.

Don't Remind Me of What I Must Do

When we're facing some dreaded task, we may push the thought down into the subconscious. This may be triggered by a dental appointment, paying a bill when we're short of money, writing an assignment for school or confronting someone who is doing something wrong. People may "forget" to do things they need to take care of. This attitude was portrayed by Scarlet O'Hara in *Gone with the Wind* when she avoided facing dreaded possibilities with the remark, "I'll think about that tomorrow."

Professional help may be required to overcome bothersome problems, dysfunctional habits or hang-ups. As we grow closer to God and through prayer, we'll ask Him for insight and wisdom to get beyond our troublesome fears. By doing so, we may find the above-mentioned "hang-ups" fading away.

Lord, increase our reverence and awe to the point that we're not afraid of anything other than displeasing You. Fill us with Your Holy Spirit until we're able to hold steady and be courageous in all situations.

SCRIPTURES TO CONSIDER

1 Corinthians 13:11
Philippians 3:13
Ephesians 3:20
Romans 15:13
Revelation 4:8b

QUESTIONS FOR DISCUSSION

1. Are there ways I continue to live in the past or wish for the "good old days?" Explain.

2. Are there memories I need to leave behind in order to move on in life? Explain.

3. One thing I dread about growing older is . . .

4. I procrastinate or put off taking care of . . .

5. Sometimes I distract myself from doing what needs to be done by . . .

6. One way I can be better prepared to face future problems is by . . .

SECTION IV
THOUGHTS CONTROL US

14

THOUGHTS IGNITE
OUR ACTIONS

It's time to focus on some good "be-attitudes"

Our thought-life is the forerunner of our words and our words typically precede our actions. Actions then solidify and define our character. God alone gives us the power to nip bad thoughts in the bud before they blossom into destructive words. And He never intends for those words to grow into poisonous fruits of our actions.

Actions will never be kept under control until we control our thoughts. If our thoughts are not disciplined, the devil knows he has access to a crack in the door for him to weasel in and defeat us through twisted thinking.

An Honest Self-Portrait

"For as he thinks within his heart, so is he" (Proverbs 23:7 AMP). Good grief! As I scrutinize my thought life, I'm not too fond of the self-portrait staring at me. There are dabs of critical attitudes, self-pity and judgments smeared here and there, along with smudges of frustration and irritation smack dab in the middle.

I'd like a new canvas to start over again, but since this is not an option, perhaps it's appropriate to resolve to live out the scripture that tells me I *can* renew my mind. *Okay Lord, bring it on.*

It's impossible to imagine how many thoughts whirl through our minds every day. I'm mortified to think what it would be like to have those thoughts posted on a bulletin board for *everyone* to read.

But how is it possible to construct a barricade every time a moving van pulls up with negative thoughts and begins to unload? I sense those thoughts are on their way to take up permanent residence in my mind. The following scripture is great, but I need the Lord to help me implement it. "Take every thought captive to make it obedient to Christ" (2 Corinthians 10:5 NIV). *Lord, bring the enemy down, exile him to parts unknown and bind him in shackles far from my mind.*

To help, I decided to start by focusing on God early mornings. I sit in my comfy overstuffed chair that faces the front door for a time of devotion and watch the early morning sunlight flickering through the beveled glass. The sun is fractured into a rainbow of colors. "Lord, come sit in the chair across the coffee table from me. Be my Light. Let the colorful plan You have for me today keep me focused on Your marching orders."

Okay, this is a start.

Don't Wait for a Crisis

All of us go through struggles in an effort to rein in our thoughts. When everything's going our way, we don't seem to need God. But when pain and hurt overwhelm us, it makes us realize how inadequate we are. In times past, it took a major crisis for me to stay focused on God.

When our son committed suicide, I wondered if there could ever be more than five minutes when the tragedy wasn't on my mind. I went to Galveston to walk along the beach. I dragged my feet through the sand, totally despondent. How could I get beyond this grief? I wandered out on the dock and looked out over the ocean to watch the waves roll in and commented, "Lord, it was such a miracle that You walked on the water. I can't comprehend it."

Deep in my spirit I felt He said, "When you're in over your head, I'll be there with you. When you're in rough waters, you will not go down. When you're between a rock and a hard place, it won't be a dead end" (Isaiah 43:2 MSG). Faced with what appeared to be a near impossibility, the Lord continued to help me focus on Him rather than the devastating tsunami flooding over my soul.

Though this tragedy happened over thirty years ago, I must still keep my defenses up so I don't get sucked back into the terrible emotions and thoughts spawned by that tragedy. At times they still assault me. I nurture my faith by repeating scriptures of God's power and His loving concern for me. It is imperative that He stand with me against Satan during these dark nights of the soul. His presence is so needed in seasons of tragedy or loss.

We Need Spiritual Discernment

I have the privilege of asking the Father to give me discernment—to distinguish between the thoughts I should allow in my mind and the ones I need to reject by posting a "Keep Out" sign. As I grow in wisdom, God gives me clear thinking on how to avoid any confusion that would keep me in turmoil and anxiety.

We've been offered God-given battle-strategy to deal with incidents that continue to pop up. It's called "wisdom." I must remind myself to requisition a large quantity every time a challenging situation appears on the scene.

Nagging suspicions, doubts and fears that plague our thinking may have bits of truth encased in them. The enemy constantly attacks our minds to infiltrate our thoughts with skewed thinking, laced with deception and lies. One formidable strategy of the devil is to catch us off-guard by climbing in bed next to us at night when we're tired. He attempts to drag us down with his all-out war against our minds.

The father of lies sets traps that lure us with deductive reasoning that's almost addictive. There's a tendency to shut out God's will from our minds with what we refer to as *logic*. The Lord may be directing us to go a certain way, but if it doesn't seem logical, we have a tendency to conclude it doesn't make good sense and disregard His GPS—**G**od's **P**rovidential **S**election—and continue going our own way.

When we consider endless alternatives, we often get confused. We hold steady only if we make sure our faith is in God alone. We're not to waver back and forth or we will become "wishy washy," like waves of the sea. (See James 1:6). Doubt wavers back and forth until unbelief washes away God's truth and His sovereignty.

God didn't create our minds to simultaneously process distinctly different trains of thought. Our thoughts flip back and forth, moment by moment. However, one of the best ways for me to keep focused is to speak aloud. The more senses involved, the more weapons are available for our defense. I raise my arms and clap my hands. In difficult times, I literally stomp my foot and announce, "Satan, you don't win! You may steal my possessions or shipwreck my plans, but you cannot ruin my attitude or snatch away my joy."

The master deceiver builds strongholds—prisons to take us captive. Once this evil tyrant shackles struggling people with bad emotions, he feeds them on rations of spoiled thinking and bitter resentments. It is dreadfully self-defeating if we give up and wave a white flag of surrender and allow him to take us prisoners. He delights in brainwashing our thinking.

Prayer and Praise

I've found the best way to prepare for battle against the enemy is through prayer and praise. These responses are my conduit to God. Prayer rises as a fragrance and captures God's attention. Praise opens the way for Him to flow into our midst.

The Holy Spirit begins to disarm our problems and remove strain and stress through this conduit. His primary gift is to splash refreshing peace over our hearts. Prayer has often been shouted in the white-water rapids of turmoil, but how much more beautiful when we listen for the Lord's whisper in quiet pools of peace and calm.

Sowing in Tears, but Reaping in Joy

Positive thoughts follow God's Word when we use the tools of faith and hope. Negative thoughts follow Satan's prompting through his attacks with fear and doubt. Praise is the best way to implement power to defeat the devil. The Bible tells us that the Lord God inhabits the praises of His people. (See Psalms 22:3 KJV) Praise flushes out negative attitudes and makes room for positive thinking.

Negative seeds planted in our mind determine the crops that

grow and bear fruit. If our lives have cultivated chaotic thoughts for years, we can't automatically begin to produce a bumper crop of peaceful fruit. It takes a concerted effort to pull out weeds of negativity. With persistence, our garden of thought life can begin to flourish.

Our mind is like soil where the seeds we scatter are the things we see, read and hear. If we're not careful, we may allow bad seeds to be planted that develop into weeds—some of which are poison. "But the seed in the good earth—these are the good hearts who seize the Word and hold on no matter what, sticking with it until there's a harvest" (Luke 8:15 MSG).

It's a slow process to renew the mind. Since our thought life has been formulated over the years, it's a challenge to repossess the areas where the devil had claimed squatter's rights. But we must make a firm commitment to accept God's Word as truth.

It seems strange, but we Christians are told we have access to the very mind of Christ (See 1 Corinthians 2:16). It takes God-given guidance and time to reprogram our thinking. When we fall short of this goal, we must try again. If we fall on our face, we know we'll get up more quickly if we *fall* down than if we deliberately *lie* down and quit.

Busyness

The mind is not to be blank, but scripture tells us, "Be still before the Lord and wait patiently for Him" (Psalms 37:7 NIV). If our mind is rabbit-trailing hither and yon, we won't hear the still, small voice of God. (See 1 Kings 19:11-12) Busyness gets us involved in a world that makes so much noise we fail to hear from our Father.

Not everything that happens in life is good and the mind has a tendency to keep flipping back to "failures, ought's and should-haves." But God is supernaturally creative by taking our brokenness and not just repairing it, but making it better than new.

Follow God-given Dreams

When God places a dream or a vision in our hearts, He not only supplies the resources and the desire to achieve this goal, but He also opens the door for us to accomplish what He's commissioned.

We must stay alert, because almost immediately after receiving an assignment from God, the devil is there with nightmares: "Do you realize all the things that could go wrong?"

He may cause us to question whether we've really heard from God or we're just "daydreaming." Our faith should be summoned to "kick in," to become the spiritual force that pushes through this sort of doubt.

"So faith comes by hearing and hearing by the word of God" (Romans 10:17 KJV). To hear our Father, it's necessary for us to learn to listen. We reinforce what we hear when we speak the wisdom of His Word aloud. When we hear His words from our own lips, we're more likely to remember them, as well as more likely to believe them.

Lord, help me to learn how to "take every thought captive." Increase my faith as I learn to listen to Your still, small voice and walk in obedience. Give me discernment to know where my thoughts are taking me and keep my eyes focused on you.

SCRIPTURES TO CONSIDER

Proverbs 22:17-19
2 Corinthians 10:4
Isaiah 43:2
Proverbs 19:8
Luke 8:15

QUESTIONS FOR DISCUSSION

1. How can we stop thinking bad thoughts?

2. Do you regularly set aside time to spend with God? What are the benefits?

3. Why is it so important to guard your thoughts?

4. Do you have any reoccurring thoughts that harass you?

5. What does it mean to have the mind of Christ?

6. How can one make sure their heart is good soil? . . .

15

ANXIETY—THE COMMON COLD OF THE PERSONALITY

A malady that makes us feel under the weather

It's frustrating when I'm undergoing a crisis and someone pats me on the shoulder and in a sanctimonious tone says, "Don't worry." That's about as comforting as it would be for me to tell a homeless person living under a bridge, "Sure hope you find a warm place to sleep tonight and something to eat." Then, turning to walk away, I leave the street person cold and hungry, with no coat or blanket. Not even a cracker to nibble on.

Anxiety is an uneasiness or distress about future uncertainties. It fills us with apprehension about all the possibilities that could come crashing down—none of them good. As anxiety accumulates, it becomes an expectant dread, a pregnant foreboding.

Worry grows out of anxiety. We're told worry borrows from tomorrow and encumbers a debt that can never be repaid. It comes with such exorbitant interest until it becomes impossible to pay off the initial debt. Anxiety may be "antsy," while fear becomes "shaky." It is like a common cold that is easy to catch, with no simple or speedy remedy.

Today often lies between a yesterday that's been squandered and a tomorrow we're not prepared for. It dumps a double "whammy" of anxiety on us, troubling our thought-life. Have you ever become restless and flit from one project to another and make a bigger mess than you started with?

We Don't Have to Earn Our Reward

Near the end of my husband's doctorate, he enrolled in a special course in counseling. His class was limited to five students. It was designed so that each student could receive close supervision. On the first day, his professor said, "Students worry about tests and final grades. In the process, they waste a great deal of time and energy because of this anxiety."

The professor issued a challenge, "You have much to learn and do in this class." He paused, and then added, "You'll each get an 'A' as long as you complete the course. Now, let's go to work." A sigh of relief was breathed throughout the room. Carey said he'd never worked so hard in a course. But it helped immensely that he and his classmates didn't have to be concerned about their final grade.

In the same sense, God has promised eternal life for His children. There's no need for us to be anxious about our final destination. But in gratitude, our motivation should prompt us to throw ourselves wholeheartedly into living the best we possibly can. "Heaven is yours as my gift to you. My Holy Spirit is my down payment (earnest, guarantee, pledge) to assure and remind you of these blessings" (Ephesians 1:13-14 AMP). Since we have these promises, there's no reason to waste time and energy in doubt and fear. We are to go out and get busy doing good in the Savior's name.

There are benefits in small amounts of anxiety. Bits of concern motivate us to get up in the morning to get to work on time. It's an incentive to study our lessons and pay our bills. However, we should maintain a careful balance so that anxiety doesn't interfere with our best efforts.

Psychological Jiggler

My mother used a pressure cooker to speed up the process of cooking food. A little gadget on top regulated the pressure building inside. We called it a "jiggler." As the pressure rose, the thing jiggled, spewed and sputtered as it released excessive pressure. If the hole that allowed the pressure to escape was clogged, it could be disastrous. The kitchen ceiling might need to be redone. Pity any person standing nearby.

Too many people find themselves living in a pressure cooker of anxiety. Frustrations and tensions build up. If there's no relief, they may explode. No one can truly know the pressure another person is experiencing, and it may be inadvisable to tell them to "hang in there."

Anxieties indicate some deadly "potion" is cooking inside: A man may be "barbecued or sizzling in stressful juices." His stomach acids may burn his insides. In extreme cases, stress and anxiety are rocks added to "rock soup" conjured up and served to him every meal.

People with high levels of anxiety may think of themselves as failures because they or others have set up unreasonable expectations for them to accomplish. That could be similar to a baseball player who expects to play a double-header on Saturday, another on Sunday—winning both days.

When our son, Paul, was in medical school, his dad told him if the pressure got too great, he should pull back. It was a relief for Paul to know he could quit if he felt he was on the verge of crashing and burning. Keeping this option in mind, he successfully completed his doctorate without excessive stress.

The Brake Is On

Anxiety impedes progress. It might be compared to trying to drive a car with the emergency brake on, which would make driving difficult. The car can't go forward without straining the engine. Neither do we work well when we're up-tight. One psychiatrist estimated that half of our energy is spent in dealing with our anxieties.

Anxiety is a "dis-ease." It stretches a person out of shape, making him uncomfortable because he's ill at ease. Research found only eight percent of what we worry about actually happens. And as people of faith, we should remember that worrying may be an indication we're afraid our problem is bigger than God.

Ways Some People Deal with Anxiety

1. Keeping busy: Some get so involved they don't have time to think about what is going on. We can follow our Master Jesus' example: "Then, because so many people were coming and going that they did not even have a chance to eat, he said to them, "Come with me by yourselves to a quiet place and get some rest" (Mark 6:31 NIV).

There are instances when staying busy may be a wise choice. Four of my five brothers were in World War II. Three of them were in dangerous war zones. The fifth was on active duty during the Korean conflict. A friend asked our mom how she handled it. She shook her head. "I raise a big garden and keep busy doing things for others."

2. Some are prone to procrastinate in dealing with situations, which adds to their anxiety. It's foolish to spend more time and energy dreading a job than actually completing it.

3. Others deny the stress and pretend they're not anxious. That's about as effective as sweeping trash under the carpet. It doesn't get rid of the dirt. When we attempt to hide things, it leaves a closet full of skeletons, a "boney-fide problem."

4. Narcotics and drugs, alcohol, tobacco and eating disorders are attempts to avoid anxious feelings. We live in an age when a large number depend on prescriptions to mask their problems. As a pharmacist, my brother-in-law owned a drug store that gave him access to many different kinds of drugs. Someone asked his wife, my sister, "What kind of tranquilizers do you take?"

She laughed, "I don't need tranquilizers."

My sister had a peace because she believed that God was at work in every situation and would work things out for her good. (See Romans 8:28) Drugs are useful and have valid purposes, but they must never be used to avoid facing the issues of life.

Anxiety may indicate we don't have an accurate concept of our Father. "We need to have no fear of someone who loves us perfectly; His perfect love for us eliminates a dread of what He might do to us. If we are afraid, it is for fear of what He might do to us, and shows that we are not fully convinced that He really loves us" (1 John 4:18 NIV).

Confession is Essential

Anxiety sneaks up behind us and grabs us by the nape of our neck. There are times when we aren't able to diagnose the root cause of a problem. However, if we find ourselves living in a state of anxiety, we've taken on God's responsibility of solving our issues.

We have failed to: "Cast all your anxieties on Him because He cares for you" (1 Peter 5:7 NIV).

When I pray, I must be sure I'm not screaming for help while refusing to turn loose of a problem I'm squeezing tight in my fist. I know that when I let go, God will handle the situation in a far better way than I can.

There are times when I've given God different options as to how He might answer my prayers. I've told Him, "A" would be great, "B" would be fine, but "C" would barely be acceptable. Then God chooses "D"—none of the above. In essence, He's saying, "You must turn it loose. Let me do what is best."

The serenity prayer that has passed down through the ages offers great wisdom and has been prayed millions of times. "Lord, grant me the courage to change the things I can change, the power to accept the things I cannot change, and the wisdom to know the difference." As I repeat this prayer, I often find anxieties begin to evaporate in the light of the Son.

Lord, give me more faith to trust You because You have all wisdom and have my best interest in mind.

SCRIPTURES TO CONSIDER

Ephesians 1:13–14
1 John 4:18
1 Peter 5:7
Mark 6:31

QUESTIONS FOR DISCUSSION

1. What makes you feel anxious? Explain.

2. Are you secure about your salvation?

3. How does worry and anxiety affect a person's performance?

4. Do you have a problem procrastinating? If so, what might you do to overcome that problem?

5. Do you have difficulty in totally releasing a problem to God? Explain.

6. Are you confident that God has your best interest in mind? Even when things go wrong?

16

TREMBLING IN MY BOOTS
A boulder of destruction

Have you ever dreamed a horrible creature was chasing you and you couldn't run or scream for help? Even after you wake up, you're still shaking with fear.

Some years ago, Carey was out of town. I heard the clock strike midnight as I sat at the dining room table counting the money I'd collected as bookkeeper for school lunches and sales from the book store. A bump outside the front door startled me. I gasped when I looked up and realized the window beside the door gave full view of the money spread on the table before me. My heart raced as I scooped up the money, crammed it in the cash box and scurried to the bathroom to hide the box in the dirty clothes hamper. I covered my mouth to keep from crying out and went into my bedroom, sat on the edge of my bed trembling. What could I do if an evil criminal was breaking in?

My heart stopped momentarily as I heard the sound of the back door squeaking open and bumping against the wall. My fears had surfaced into reality! I grabbed a marble book-end from the night-stand and waited . . . Nothing. Perhaps the intruder had taken off his shoes and was sneaking down the hall in his sock feet.

My imagination went ballistic as horrible thoughts raced through my mind. Is this how my life would end? When I could stand it no longer, I crept out into the hallway, pressed my back against the wall and eased toward the open area that led to the back door. I saw the opened door and my heart pounded—almost exploding. But as my eyes scanned the room, there was no one there. Step by shaky step, I reached the door and found it still locked. "Oh, thank you Lord."

I had not completely closed the door and a gust of wind had blown it open. My fears were unfounded, but they were as terrifying as if someone had actually come as a threat to my life.

Fear has a tendency to demolish whatever walls of faith we've constructed, as well as destroying our trust that the Lord will take care of us. Sudden fear may be spawned and flourish when we think of the worst possible tragedy that may happen.

I'm grateful that as my faith grows, my fears lose their power to control me. I will probably never reach the point God intended when He spoke, "Perfect love casts out all fear." It's my goal, however, to ask for His grace to so completely surround me that I *know* without a shadow of a doubt, He will bring good from every fearful thing that happens.

Fear can be fatal. Highly superstitious people in third world countries die when a voodoo curse is placed on them. Here in our country, we speak of being "scared to death" or "our heart skipping a beat" when we're afraid. Fear quickens the pulse and knots the stomach. It's a jangling alarm set off by anticipation of danger, pain or disaster. Dread and terror are the fertilizers that cause fear to develop into a monster. When coupled with imagination, fear becomes full-fledged panic.

Lance the Fear

When I was ten years old, two painful boils rose up on my leg. My dad examined them and told me they'd have to be lanced in order to drain them. My panic rose from a two to a ten as he leaned near with a single edged razor blade to slice through the festering sores. However, he moved quickly and cut the boils open so my leg could begin healing. My worst fear of dying of pain passed.

Since then, I've had several occasions when sore issues needed "lanced" (dealt with) so the underlying problem could begin to heal. Painful? Yes, but there are times when the Great Physician needs to take His scalpel and perform surgery.

Many have a fear of losing control. That is why there are an increasing number of young girls who are fearful of becoming overweight. Some become anorexic or bulimic by eating little or purging themselves after they have eaten. This is the one thing they can control in their obsession to lose weight. Their thinking has become so distorted they see themselves as fat, regardless of what the scales tell them.

The daughter of a friend went into a treatment center for eating disorders. At the time, she only weighed 79 pounds. Another girl who checked into the center looked as if she might weigh still less. As a reaction, my friend's daughter tried to commit suicide. The fear of loss of control can have deadly repercussions.

Invitation

The only legitimate fear is to "fear God and keep His commandments, for this is the whole duty of man" (Ecclesiastes 12:13 NIV). As long as I stay underneath God's umbrella of protection, my fears are unwarranted. We need to abandon our fears, trusting our Father to hold our hand.

Thank God, He has given us a process to counterbalance the weighty load of fear by helping us recall times when He's brought us through dreadful situations. "Come to me. Get away with me and you'll recover your life. I'll show you how to take a real rest. Walk with me and work with me—watch how I do it. Learn the unforced rhythms of grace. I won't lay anything heavy or ill-fitting on you. Keep company with me and you'll learn to live freely and lightly" (Matthew 11:28-30 MSG).

This invitation has wondrous implications to those of us shackled by heavy chains of fear—that have the potential to immobilize us. We've used the expression of being "scared stiff," implying we're unable to move ahead.

On a few occasions, it may be wise to remain perfectly still when overcome with fear. If we came upon a rattlesnake coiled to strike, it might be a good idea to "freeze" and wait until it crawls away.

The Bible tells a wonderful story about Elisha's servant who was very fearful as they faced a large army. "Elisha prayed, 'O Lord, open his eyes so that he may see.' The Lord then opened the servant's eyes so that he looked and saw the hills full of horses and chariots of fire all around Elisha" (2 Kings 6:17 NIV). How comforting to know that the one that surrounds us is far more powerful than all the forces of hell.

God's Solution to Fear

There would be a legitimate reason to fear if we were left with nothing but our own resources as a defense. Our personal strength and wisdom are grossly inadequate to deal with life's traumas. There are 366 references in the Bible where we're told not to fear. That's enough for every day of the year with one left over. How encouraging to know, "We are hard pressed on every side, but not crushed; perplexed, but not in despair; persecuted, but not abandoned; struck down, but not destroyed" (2 Corinthians 4:8-9 NIV).

I am forever grateful that we have other Christians to come alongside us. God didn't intend for us to be the only soldier on the battlefield to fight the enemy. Together we can proclaim triumphantly with these fellow soldiers in God's army, "The battle belongs to the Lord" (2 Chronicles 20:15 NIV).

Decades ago my dad was digging a cistern to catch rain water that ran off the house. He and a hired worker hit rock and decided to use dynamite to blast through the barrier. A ladder leaned against the side of the cistern where they could climb out before the dynamite exploded.

They lit the fuse and the "hired hand" scrambled up the ladder. Just as he was climbing over the edge, the ladder broke. The man clung to the edge at the top where another man grabbed his hands to help pull him out. Dad pushed on his feet to shove him up over the top. My father was left behind with the fuse on the dynamite burning shorter by the second. It was too late to stomp it out. I'm sure Dad's heart pounded with fear, although he never cried out. He simply sat down beside the explosive, prepared to die.

Suddenly, the man who'd escaped threw down a rope. The two men pulled Dad over the edge just as the powerful dynamite exploded. He was so close to the explosion it blew rocks up over his head. He'd faced his fear and remained calm even when death seemed inevitable.

On another occasion, when Dad was cutting wood with a gasoline-powered circular saw, he picked up a crooked stick to cut in two. The stick twisted and threw his fingers into the saw. One finger was completely severed. My sister and I screamed in horror as Dad looked at where his index finger had been and calmly remarked, "It's off." He showed no fear as he cleaned his hand before Mom drove him to the doctor.

My father became my role model of one who could face his fear and continue to trust God with his life and future.

The Octopus of Fear

Imagine fear being represented as tentacles on an octopus. Each tentacle would be powerful enough to squeeze the life out of us. If we are plagued with more than one of these fears, it compounds the problem. These eight illustrations are not exclusive, but give an idea of some of the concerns that can crush us and take our breath away.

1. FEAR OF SICKNESS OR DEATH.
2. FEAR OF BEING INADEQUATE.
3. FEAR OF LOSS OF CONTROL.
4. FEAR OF LACK OF MONEY OR FINANCIAL SECURITY.
5. FEAR OF BEING REJECTED. (THIS MAY HAPPEN BECAUSE WE'VE BEEN REJECTED IN THE PAST.)
6. FEAR OF BEING ALONE.
7. FEAR OF FAILURE.
8. FEAR OF MAN. (THIS MAY HAPPEN BECAUSE WE ARE MORE CONCERNED ABOUT PLEASING MAN THAN PLEASING GOD.)

Lord, help me to so believe that Your perfect love casts out fear, that I can relax as if I were securely sitting in Your lap, held in Your arms.

SCRIPTURES TO CONSIDER

Ecclesiastes 12:13
Matthew 11:28-30
2 Kings 6:16-17
2 Corinthians 4:8-9
2 Chronicles 20:15

QUESTIONS FOR DISCUSSION

1. Have you had times when your fears were unfounded? Explain

2. Have you learned lessons as a result of a difficult situation? Explain.

3. Tell of a time when you faced your fears. What was the result?

4. Does the problem of trying to please people affect you?

5. Explain the difference you see between being courageous and being foolish.

6. Do you have any specific fears? Discuss.

SECTION V
BE GOOD TO YOURSELF

17

SELF-ESTEEM OR SELF-IMPORTANCE

I can't love others if I despise myself

Conception was intended to come as the result of an act of love. God planned for this newly conceived life to give and receive love. An accurate understanding of this is essential if we're to have the right perspective of ourselves and others. God designed us to have a self-image which isn't too high or too low.

Our self-image changes, not only from day to day, but from hour to hour. My sister woke up feeling good about herself until she got in the car to go to the store and started backing out of the garage—without opening the door. Crunch! Not too smart. It's easy to be distracted because we're thinking of other things.

Our train of thought is constantly challenged with myriads of circumstances that either give us confidence or bombard our minds with doubt. At times we feel self-assured and content about who we are, which causes our self-image to soar. But when one or more adverse conditions broadside us, our self-esteem plummets—leaving us confused, wondering whether we're of any earthly good.

Inaccurate Evaluation of Ourselves

If I put on rose-colored glasses to take a look at myself, I may declare, "I'm just fine." But in the process, I may decide no one else looks or acts right. When my opinion is based on pride and arrogance, I put "me" on a pedestal, where I look down on those surrounding me.

A selfish person is self-absorbed. In trying to fill his own needs, he snatches what he can from everything and everyone. In his quest to look important, his overindulgence causes his ego to become overweight and ugly. His life is based on "me, my and mine." Humility has been swept out the door. If a man becomes his own god, he'll be the only one left to brag about how great he is. God has been crowded out—the very resource that could have enriched his life with a healthy self-esteem.

God Intends for Us to Feel Good About Ourselves

God hates selfishness. "I warn everyone among you not to estimate and think of himself more highly than he ought—not to have an exaggerated opinion of his own importance" (Romans 12:3 AMP). However, God has His own prerequisites for us to be encouraged about how we've been created.

Legalistic religious teachers often emphasize obedience to God and helping others, but fail to teach the significance of loving ourselves. If we don't feel good about who we are, our countenance won't glow and our hearts will be too heavy to reach out in compassion to others. Self-esteem is the foundation on which to build a better world.

A blessed self-image doesn't come floating down on a cloud. We're in trouble if we mope around doing nothing, waiting for people to dump positive accolades on us. When we're complacent, sit and stare into space, we may be a prime target for the devil to come and use our mind his workshop.

He's always looking for opportunities to tempt us to conjure up bad attitudes toward others, as well as dumping in defeating thoughts about our own self-worth. A good person who wouldn't think of doing something evil may allow degrading thoughts about himself to settle in and take up permanent residence in his mind. You possibly know of beautiful women that continue to think of themselves as ugly.

We must search God's Word to realize how deeply our Father loves us. Each of us is a unique design, especially created for His selected purpose. Knowing this should wrap us in satisfaction and contentment.

The Flip Side of Feeling Too Haughty and Proud

Some have convinced themselves they don't measure up. They put themselves down with such remarks as, "I'm not really good enough. I don't deserve God's love or salvation." Since we typically remember the worst things we've done, the enemy recycles those thoughts. He contrives ways to convince us God will always hold those charges against us and we'll never get beyond those failures.

When a person doesn't feel good about himself, he may conclude that others feel the same way. If he resorts to self-deprecation, he'll feel his life is of little value.

Others play self-defeating psychological games. They rehearse their wrongs, faults, weaknesses, sins and inadequacies. The longer they dwell on their bad encounters with life, the lower the self-esteem drops. Bad feelings of self-worth may cause one to conclude, "If others knew me like I know me, they wouldn't like me either."

This may lead to the false conclusion that God has also rejected them. Defeated, they turn away from God and His Word. It is almost as if to say, "Since He couldn't possibly love me, I'll show Him. I don't have to have His love, and furthermore, I won't love Him."

When looking in the mirror, this person wishes he looked different. He looks at his home and longs for something better. Peace and contentment are never satisfied, because cravings become insatiable. This type of person is constantly on the look-out for something he can drag into his life to cling to. He develops a form of hoarding which morphs into clutter and trash.

It's Time to Take a Look

For a healthy self-esteem, we must understand its origin, the seed from which it sprouts and the conditions under which it grows. With this perspective, we'll be able to accurately judge ourselves.

We can be frustrated with our weaknesses, despise our mistakes and sins, and still live rich lives by understanding that God has put us together so we can successfully accomplish the plans He has for us. Love of self is an absolute prerequisite for loving others. If a person doesn't have his own bucket filled with love, he has nothing to pour into the lives of others.

When Jesus tells us to love ourselves, it doesn't come from a selfish motivation. Healthy self-esteem and selfishness spring from different roots, producing radically different fruit. Selfish roots grow inward, focused on *us*. Self-esteem that is rooted in what the Word says about us causes us to grow upward and outward—focused on God and others. The fruit of the Spirit growing in our lives is evidence of God's love and acceptance. That makes me feel good about myself.

Biblical Reasoning

It is God's design for a man to love and take care of his body. "Even as husbands should love their wives as (being in a sense) their own bodies. He who loves his own wife loves himself. For no man ever hated his own flesh, but nourishes and carefully protects and cherishes it, as Christ does the church" (Ephesians 5:28-29 AMP). With this in mind, we're given permission to pamper ourselves with a bit of TLC.

"Don't you know that you yourselves are God's temple and that God's Spirit lives in you?" (1 Corinthians 3:16 NIV). The temple in the Old Testament was a structure where people admired the outside. God lived in the Holy Place—the innermost part. The temple in the New Testament is our body, and God is to live in the innermost part there, within our hearts and easy access. This implies we have an awesome responsibility to take care of our bodies emotionally, physically and spiritually.

In the physical body, each part notifies the other of its needs. The stomach tells the head when to give it food and a stubbed toe calls for a hand to massage it gently for comfort. In a similar way, the body of Christ is to express and reach out to the needs of each other.

A healthy self-esteem is a wholesome acceptance of gifts and at-tributes God has given us. This frees us from preoccupation with self and gives us the time and opportunity to reach out in a meaningful way to anyone around. "Live freely, animated and motivated by

God's Spirit. Then you won't feed the compulsions of selfishness. For there is a root of sinful self-interest in us that is at odds with a free Spirit ..." (Galatians 5:16-17 MSG).

The mature Christian is one who is content, not only with what he has, but also who he is and where he stands in life. When he sees an opportunity to grow, he's ready to step up to the plate to become more competent and strong. He's not only available, but eager to share his blessed life with others.

Self-love is Enhanced by God and Others

Jesus emphasized the biblical basis of self-esteem by listing two concepts of major importance: "Love the Lord your God with all your heart and with all your soul and with all your mind.' This is the first and greatest commandment. And the second is like it: 'Love your neighbor as yourself.' All the Law and the Prophets hang on these two commandments (Matthew 22:37-39 NIV). This scripture leaves no doubt about the need to love ourselves.

The love of God is primary, but it is directly connected to the second law. It is essential for God to have top priority in our lives, but He nails the point by adding: "All the other commandments and all the demands of the prophets stem from these *two* laws and are fulfilled if you obey them. Keep only these and you will find that you are obeying all the others" (Matthew 22:40 TLB). We find a bonding cycle of love between the Father, others and self.

Man feels best about himself when his actions are not solely for his own benefit, but in helping others as well. God furnishes us with the high octane fuel of the Holy Spirit, which is capable not only of getting us off ground zero, but is powerful enough to lift others up with us. I have fond memories of a song we sang in church: *Love Lifted Me.* Love lifts a heavy heart. It lightens the load and elevates our spirits while it beckons others to come on board.

I invited three of my little granddaughters, age three, five and eight to come to my house to make Christmas cookies. We made a horrific mess with flour, "sprinkles" and icing splattered from head to toe. As we finished and stood admiring the decorated cookies, the five-year-old announced, "This is the best day of my life." Though I was worn out when they left, I felt good about what we'd done and, as I tackled the chore of cleaning up the mess, I had a smile on my face.

People ask, "What is the most important thing in life?" The answer isn't based on church activities—such as singing, praying, giving or even Bible study. God's greatest commandments deal with relationships. Let the cross be a symbol of our relationships. The vertical beam represents our lives pointing up to God, while the horizontal beam represents our arms reaching out to embrace others.

Self-love Is Enhanced By Others

The head of the Physical Education and Recreation department at the University of Wyoming encouraged me to get my master's degree in "recreation," because he said no woman at that university had gotten a degree in that field. I took his challenge. During registration, he introduced me to my professors with the statement, "I'm bringing you a straight "A" student." I pulled him aside and told him, "I've never been a straight "A" student." He countered with, "You will be." That reinforced my belief that the world needs encouragers. Strangely, I *almost* lived up to his expectations and only made one "B" in graduate school. (I worked hard!)

We're motivated when someone believes in us. It empowers us if we think of God sitting in the stands as a whole cheering section. His encouragement is the biggest factor in building self-esteem.

And thinking about encouragement, I'm prone to think about Barnabas, Paul's friend. His name means encourager. I think I'd like to be known as a *Barnabess*.

Basis for Self-esteem

If a man is to embrace this reassuring attitude of loving himself, he must realize he's made in God's image and even contains a spark of His divine nature. "Let us make mankind in our image, in our likeness . . . (Genesis 1:26-27 NIV).

Our self-esteem catapults into great feelings about ourselves when we begin to fathom how much our heavenly Father loves us—enough to call us His children. It is sad when one doesn't know God, much less accept the fact he has been given the privilege of being adopted as His child. As His children, we anticipate an inheritance beyond anything we can imagine. After He comes again, we will see Him as He really is. This is breath-taking.

When God put our DNA together, He included elements of godliness. My prayer is for the Holy Spirit to blow on those sparks until they burst into a flame of righteousness.

It is interesting to see older couples who actually begin to look like one another after years of living together. I pray the longer I nurture a relationship with God, the more I'll look like Him. "And we all, who with unveiled faces contemplate the Lord's glory, are being transformed into his image with ever-increasing glory, which comes from the Lord, who is the Spirit" (2 Corinthians 3:18 NIV).

It pleases me to realize that though we're far from perfect, we can look at ourselves in the mirror and confidently affirm, "God is not finished with me yet!" We rest in the deep assurance of knowing whose child we are and that He will continue to work on us until our last fleeting breath. Okay, Lord, go ahead and use the sandpaper!

Father, give us a true perspective of ourselves. Build our confidence to the point of accomplishing everything You've assigned for us to do. But keep us from being prideful, because we know we're only doing what's expected. Thank You for providing us with everything we need to be the best we can possibly be.

SCRIPTURES TO CONSIDER

Matthew 22:33–40
Romans 3:21–31
Romans 4:1–8
Romans 5:6–11
Romans 7:15 – 8:4
Galatians 4:1–11

QUESTIONS FOR DISCUSSION

1. Name at least three things that make you feel good about yourself.

2. List things that God's blessed you with recently.

3. When people first meet me, their initial impression is . . .

4. People who know me best say that I . . .

5. I would feel better about myself if . . .

18

PERSONALITY PLUS

Investing your assets

People often lump the definition of personality into two major categories: good or bad. These broad descriptions give little insight into a person's disposition. If we only have this scant knowledge of a person, we'll walk away wondering, what do they mean by *good* or *bad*?

Probing deeper, we may discover the person has a "stubborn streak" or is a "control freak." Perhaps he's "thoughtful and kind." We tend to search for a trait that sets him apart from others. The attributes of one's personality help determine the person's character, and his character determines his destiny.

Our personalities are often reflected in our mood which is often like the weather—ever changing and often unpredictable.

- Sometimes we're windy and full of hot air.
- Other days our mood is overcast and dark, creating an atmosphere of depression.
- When we are warm and sunshiny, those around us blossom.
- When our temperature is hot, our anger boils over to blast those nearby.
- The dark clouds in our own lives may cause it to rain on another's parade.
- If our communication is confusing and unclear, it creates a foggy relationship.
- When our thoughts are clear and bright, we invite others to come outside and play, where we enjoy being together.

Our personality is revealed through moods like being grumpy, cheerful, depressed or loving. Walt Disney defined the personality of each of the seven dwarfs by naming them by a characteristic that identified them. Though we're born with a certain disposition, thankfully we have the ability to make modifications, to utilize the wisdom and self-control God provides. "Why don't you choose to be led by the Spirit and so escape the erratic compulsions of a law-dominated existence?" (Galatians 5:18 MSG).

Don't be Two-faced

A person is considered to be two-faced if he gives a certain impression one time and a contrasting one the next. Less desirable personality traits often show up inside the walls of one's home. The sister of a famous preacher remarked, "He is adored by others because he treats them as if they were special, true heirs of God. But at home, he is rude and inconsiderate of his family. His children are beginning to rebel against him, and in the process, they're turning against the God He claims to uphold as a standard."

As Christians, we're told to persevere in maintaining a Christ-like attitude. "There should be a consistency that runs throughout our words and actions. For Jesus doesn't change, yesterday, today, or tomorrow" (Hebrews 13:7 MSG). If we have "road rage" behind the wheel of a car, our Jesus bumper sticker drags the reputation of Christianity in the dirt.

Different aspects of our personality may be exposed when we're faced with trauma, excitement or challenges. Hard times can develop substance to our character and at the same time, expose the root system of our nature. "Oh that my steps might be steady, keeping to the course you set; Then I'd never have any regrets in comparing my life to your counsel" (Psalms119:6 MSG).

"The first man Adam became a living being—an individual personality; (the last Adam, Christ) became a life-giving Spirit—restoring the dead to life"(1 Corinthians 15:45 AMP). It is amazing that we too have the ability to inject life into dead circumstances, especially if we look at miserable experiences as opportunities to learn.

Even our mistakes can be the bottom end of the learning curve where we can look up to see how to climb back to the top. If we continue to listen to God, He'll teach us that good can come from a bad situation.

Though a person believes his hopes have been burned to the ground, he can dig through the ashes to resurrect life to form a beneficial lesson.

A television program featured the story of a young boy with great potential who loved to learn. He was bullied, called names, and teased unmercifully because of his desire to excel. When he was eleven years old, the pain of rejection became so intense, he hung himself. His family dug through the ashes of this devastating experience and began a crusade against bullying. With sterling characteristics of God-like qualities, they took what Satan meant for evil and are bringing good in their efforts to end bullying.

Look for the Good

We have the opportunity to play a vital role in developing good personalities. When we emphasize one redeeming quality in a person's life, it helps that segment to blossom. We're also likely to see growth in other areas. Confidence spreads and strengthens other facets of a person's character.

Confidence, like yeast, takes the initiative to spread in a warm atmosphere.

When our son was in the first grade, I was amazed at the effort those young students put forth to excel. I mentioned this remarkable observation to the teacher, and she explained, "From the first day of school, I begin to look for any special quality a student can control and develop. I avoid things like pretty eyes, but emphasize attributes such as their spontaneous smile or their kindness to others." She chuckled, "Sometimes I have to search to find a positive characteristic, but when I do, it affects the child's whole attitude. They often begin excel in other areas as well."

God-like Lives

"I came that they may have and enjoy life, and have it in abundance—to the full, till it overflows" (John.10:10 AMP). In seeking for this abundant life of which Jesus speaks, we find many transformations come as a result of how we respond to the challenges we run up against in life. Whether it is Abraham, Moses or the Apostle Paul, we'd do well to remember none of these God-fearing people lived trouble-free lives. Their perseverance, however, produced remarkable examples that have echoed down through the ages.

It would have been interesting to have known Enoch, because we're told he walked with God and then God took him (See Genesis 5:24). When we walk alongside another, it's as if we're united—arm in arm—standing in agreement with common beliefs, words and actions. Since we were created to be companions of God, it well may be that the Lord called for Enoch to come on home to move closer to Him, to be His special friend.

In Acts 13:22 David is described as a person *after* God's own heart. That may be interpreted in two ways—either he pursued God's heart or he had a heart like God's. In either case, this was a touching endorsement.

As we look in the Old Testament, especially in Psalms, we find David riding a roller-coaster of emotions. At one moment he's yelling at God, and the next he's falling on his face in praise and adoration. David was a man who experienced and expressed the full gamut of emotions—from shouting hallelujahs to crying out in despair. In the worst of times, David voiced his complaints, but concluded "Yet I will praise Him."

This remarkable man never developed lead poisoning by biting the bullet and remaining quiet.

David sinned in the worst ways, but confessed and responded with deep repentance and sorrow. Nathan, the prophet, knew he needed to confront him about his sin of adultery with Bathsheba and then arranging for her husband to be killed in battle. David didn't flinch until Nathan gave him an illustration of someone taking a man's only pet lamb and slaughtering it. David was incensed and demanded the man be punished. Nathan nailed him with, "You are the man."

Because David was king, He could have banished Nathan or sent him to the gallows. Instead, King David took ownership of his sin and repented in deep contrition. The core of David's personality seemed to have been molded around his determination to take the shattered pieces of his life and lift them up for God to forgive and heal.

These godly men had pure hearts exuding with a continuous flow of love. Each appeared to have a personality that reflected Christ living in them. "Christ in you, the hope of glory" (Colossians 1:27 NIV). This short scripture reverberates with powerful implications.

A Servant's Heart

What would it have been like to "hang out" with Jesus as He ministered to people? He was loving and compassionate most of the time, but harsh when He confronted religious hypocrites. His personality attracted thousands, yet when He spoke truth, it created a sharp division between those who followed Him and those who would turn against Him. Each faction was adamant in their convictions. No one lingered in the shadows or gray areas of doubt. Jesus said people were either for Him or against Him. *Lord, help us live our lives in a definitive way by standing firm with you.*

Dare to picture Jesus and his disciples in the upper room in Jerusalem. Jesus had served the Last Supper to his chosen twelve, explaining that the bread symbolized His body and the wine represented His blood. Toward the end of the meeting, His disciples were intimidated when He insisted He would wash their feet.

The profundity of Jesus' personality was broadcast as totally God-like when He knelt and washed the feet of Judas, whom He knew would betray Him. Can't you imagine grieving tears falling on the feet of the betrayer as our Lord realized that of one of His own would turn against Him? Jesus became the epitome of unconditional love—even toward the one whose vile sin of betrayal would result in Him being beaten, ridiculed and nailed to a cross as if He were one of the worst of criminals.

As Judas left to betray his Lord, Jesus gives the others a charge. "I give you a new commandment, that you should love one another; just as I have loved you, so you too should love one another. By this shall all (men) know that you are my disciples, if you love one another—if you keep on showing love among yourselves" (John 13:34-35 AMP).

Jesus followed through to the end, leaving a legacy of unparalleled examples. He even asked God to forgive the very ones who had beaten him unmercifully and crammed a crown of thorns on His head. After forcing Him to carry the cross to Golgotha, they nailed spikes through His hands and feet, and then jammed the cross into the ground. The jolts and jarring of this persecution had to have caused unimaginable pain. After all that, Jesus asked God to forgive these perpetrators so they might receive an inheritance and live as His friends, alongside Him throughout eternity. Our Lord has been the only perfect match for God's personality—the personification of love. Blessed be His Holy Name.

Father, never let me be two-faced, but rather teach me to be consistent in following you with a singleness of vision and a Christ-like attitude every step of the way.

SCRIPTURES TO CONSIDER

1 Corinthians 15:45
Galatians 5:16
Hebrews 13:7
Malachi 3:7
Colossians 1:27
John 13:34–35

QUESTIONS FOR DISCUSSION

1. In five words or less, describe your personality as you see it.

2. What kind of mood are you generally in?

3. How can Christ be seen in you as your hope of glory? Explain.

4. Do you know anyone who bullies or manipulates to get their way? Do *you* do this?

5. Who, in the Bible, other than Jesus, would you have liked to have "hung out" with? Why?

6. Do you have a personality trait you would like to change? Explain.

SECTION VI
DEALING WITH
WRONG CHOICES

19

GUILT—THE GANGRENE
OF THE PERSONALITY

Don't leave the Drain-O in the pipes

A four-year-old neighbor playing with a brick tossed it in the air and ducked. You guessed it. The brick hit him on the head! It sounds dumb, but in a sense, this is how many people handle guilt. They pick out a "chunk" of guilt from their sack, some failure or sin from the past and toss it around in their minds. It crashes down on their heads, creating painful wounds and damaging their egos.

How Well Did You Sleep?

People frequently carry a heavy load of guilt that could be compared to a bag of rocks. It's pathetic, but some not only carry this load throughout the day, but also fail to put the bag away when they crawl into bed at night. The bag is right there next to them under the covers. Insomnia disturbs them as one bumps into the lumps, dragging them further into the dumps!

No wonder that person wakes up weary, dreading the thought of having to carry those dreadful rocks again.

The load one carries may not be made up of literal stones, but rather emotional or psychological weights that represent guilt. We can symbolize guilt as the emotional stones he's accumulated over the years. It becomes an even greater burden if he picks up more rocks of concern of things that possibly lie ahead. (Guilt looks backward while fear looks ahead.)

Many of these rocks represent things we should or shouldn't have done, or unwise decisions we've made. I've had difficulty turning loose of a memory of my oldest son who took his own life. I remember him coming home excited when he was in fifth grade because his class had elected me as home room mother. I told him I was too busy, and though he begged me, I refused to accept the nomination.

I regret being unwilling to do something Rick really wanted. I added this memory to other times when I failed to give him top priority in my life. I've kicked myself for being a "bad mom." I still find myself praying for God to forgive me for my lack of loving commitment to meet Rick's needs. I know I've been forgiven, but Satan continues to try to sneak those rocks back in my bag, though he has no right. "For the accuser of our brothers and sisters, who accuses them before our God day and night, has been hurled down" (Revelation 12:10 NIV).

If we allow them, destructive thoughts sweep through our minds. This happens as we reach back into our memory bank, pull out rocks and polish them by reliving disturbing incidents. A memory is often multidimensional, accompanied by pain and embarrassment. Anger and bitterness may also grow out of guilt.

These feelings of guilt intensify when each accusing memory links with others that are dredged up to make us feel we're a failure. By rehashing bad memories, it's like picking scabs off our wounds to see if they're healing. It leaves an open sore that's likely to become infected. If the healing balm of Jesus' blood is not applied, people are in danger of developing "psychological gangrene." The self-image becomes infected with shame and failure.

Clean out the Pipes

My neighbor became frustrated when her kitchen sink backed up and her dishwasher overflowed with a sloppy mess that spread the dirty water into two other rooms. She called a plumber who came and discovered she'd crammed too many things in her garbage disposal and failed to flush it out. This added guilt to her negative thinking. Anger became a part of these disturbing emotions because of the price the plumber charged to unclog her sink.

As poisons build up in our physical bodies each day, there's a natural process of elimination that utilizes lungs, sweat glands, kidneys and bowels. If any of these essential organs ceases to function, toxic poisons build and can lead to illness or even death. *Thank you, Lord, you've provided everything we need to rid us of poisonous guilt.*

Guilt is a God-given emotion that calls our attention to the fact that there are things in our lives that need to be taken out. That's good. These red flags let us know something's gone awry. If we hang onto these feelings over a period of time without resolving the issue, they clog the flow of healthy thinking.

Since we live as fallible humans in a fallen world, we inevitably do and say things that leave guilty trails. Though these were meant to prick our hearts, they were never intended as punishment that would stab or mutilate our sense of well-being.

It would be wonderful if we had a handle for a quick solution that would flush these memories away. Regrettably, it's usually a slow grinding process to get rid of these rocks. Only the consistent sandpapering of God's grace totally removes them from our souls. There are times we think we've taken care of them, only to find Satan has sneaked in and layered them with more accusations.

Several options are possible when dealing with guilt: suppress, repress, or confess wrongs that have been the source. Only the last of these options—confession, is God-ordained. Only our Redeemer can totally free us of our shame. Through confession, we agree with Him that what we've done is wrong. When that happens, the Living Water flows freely to wash away the stains of guilt.

We have the sole responsibility of starting the process. It's as if we find God nearby with folded hands, waiting until we admit we don't have the ability to clear the air or "drain the pipes" of guilt alone.

Beasts of Burdens

In some areas of the world, camels are widely used as beasts of burdens. At the end of the day, a camel is made to kneel down so his load can be removed to allow him to get comfortable—to eat, rest and sleep. The following morning, the master has the animal kneel down for him to receive the load he's to carry that day. If he's burdened with too heavy a weight, he'll be worn out, having little strength to go on. On the other hand, if the load is too light, the camel will never grow stronger. A sensible nomad is careful to place the proper load on his beast of burden.

We too can kneel each night to ask our Master to remove the weights that have been piled on us during the day, so our body, mind and spirit can be restored. The next morning, we kneel before Him, trusting He will give us the proper load for the day, not so heavy that we're overburdened, but not so light we remain weak or become lazy.

Dump the Load

If people have carried their guilt since childhood, the wasted time and energy is enormous. The rocks have become such a part of a person's life-style they appear to be glued to their personality like barnacles on a ship. The more traumatic the experiences and the longer the rocks are carried, the more difficult it is to pry them loose.

At Hidden Manna, our retreat center, we often had guests go out onto the dock by the lake. There, each participant was given a stack of rocks to throw into the water. Each rock was to represent some guilt they'd been carrying. One woman spent most of the afternoon tossing her rocks in the lake. Two weeks later, her husband called. "I think my wife came back and waded out in the lake and recovered her discarded load."

In a similar way, some of us find ourselves repeatedly picking up the same rocks time and again. We've failed to turn loose of them in order for the Father to take them far away and bury them. "You will again have compassion on us; you will tread our sins underfoot and hurl all our iniquities into the depths of the sea" (Micah 7:19 NIV). And, as Corrie ten Boom added, "He puts up a *no fishing* sign."

Father, build our faith until we trust You to take our confessed sins and totally forgive and forget them. Teach us how to accept that forgiveness. Though we still remember the sin, it will have lost its power to control us.

SCRIPTURES TO CONSIDER

Revelations 12:10
Micah 7:19
Matthew 11:28
Psalms 32:3-5

QUESTIONS FOR DISCUSSION

1. Do you have guilt that bothers you? What can you do?

2. What harm comes from rehashing bad things that have happened in life? What's the solution?

3. What is God's provision for guilt? Why do you think it is not practiced more?

4. Do you have things that may come up in the future that you dread?

5. How does Satan harass us with bad memories?

6. What is the purpose of our conscious? Describe the right and wrong use of it.

20

SPIRITUAL CASTOR OIL

How do I get to the garbage dump?

Guilty feelings can only be flushed out by the spiritual *catharsis* of confession. Confession is the God-given prerequisite to purging sin. Through this act we're awarded the healing gift of forgiveness. "Therefore confess your sins to each other and pray for each other so that you may be healed. The prayer of a righteous person is powerful and effective" (James 5:16 NIV).

Confession opens a package of forgiveness from the throne room of God, sent by the way of the cross. It is only through this cleansing power that we're counted worthy to walk alongside our perfect Redeemer.

When we hang on to guilt, we must be aware that these defeating accusations don't come from God. We know the "accuser of the brethren" wants to defeat us and rob us of any relief God has for us.

Each time a tiny bit of guilt attempts to slither into our minds, we have the blessed privilege of seeking God's support. "Submit yourselves, then, to God. Resist the devil, and he will flee from you" (James 4:7 NIV). Submission, coupled with praise, assures us that the enemy won't stick around to listen. He hates to hear anyone praise Almighty God.

Being relieved of guilt is often dealt with effectively in Christ-centered groups. People experience tremendous relief when they share in the process of "unloading rocks." A participant confesses by agreeing with God that what he's done is wrong. He further admits the sin of keeping his focus on the wrong he's committed, rather than on God.

At our retreat center, we have another option in dealing with sin and guilt. Each attendee is asked to write down situations he feels guilty about and then confess one thing on his list to the group. As we share each other's troubles and problems, we are acting out of obedience to what the Lord has commanded. No one is forced to reveal anything that it too painful or personal, but if a participant chooses to do so, they typically experience relief from being transparent rather than feeling naked and exposed. At the completion of this exercise, we take the papers out to an altar on the hill to burn as a visual symbol to show sin and shame are reduced to ashes—to be blown away.

God's Forgiveness Is Far Greater than Man's

A local drunk went to a revival, made a commitment to Christ and was baptized. The congregation rejoiced. A couple of weeks later, when he'd been unable to find a job, he got drunk again. The following Sunday he went before the church in tears to repent and ask for prayers. Several commented, "I didn't figure that old drunk could stay sober." The new believer was discouraged about falling off the wagon, but continued to search for work.

A month passed before he gave in to temptation and went on another drinking binge. He went before the church again to repent. Many other members joined the first group and expressed their doubt, "He's been drinking too long. He'll always be a sot."

He held steady for several months before he got drunk once more. He left the bar and went to his apartment, fell on his face and cried out, "Lord, I promised I'd be faithful, but Father, I've done it again!" God's loving reply was, "Done what?" *Lord, give me such understanding of Your unconditional forgiveness until I'm no longer judgmental. Help me stick to a commitment to forgive myself and others seventy times seven.*

The White Stone

In ages past, slave-owners would take an awl, punch a hole in his servant's ear, and attach a black stone as a symbol that he was a slave. If the slave ever removed the black stone, he'd be sentenced to death. If at some point he was set free or able to buy his freedom, the master would remove the stone and replace it with a white one as evidence to the world that this slave was a free man. "To him who overcomes, to him I will give *some* of the hidden manna, and I will give him a white stone, and a new name written on the stone which no one knows but he who receives it" (Revelation 1:17 NASB) Believers accept the white stone is a reminder that we have been set free from the bondage of sin.

At Hidden Manna, we often counsel with a person who needs to be rid of his "black rocks" of guilt. They're given the assurance that our Savior bought their freedom. They're no longer a slave to sin and there's no reason for them to continue to carry that cursed burden. We give them a small white stone to remind them of their freedom.

Some have carried those smooth white stones for years. One woman had hers made into a locket. "I am using these everyday examples, because in some ways you are still weak. You used to let the different parts of your body be slaves of your evil thoughts. But now you must make every part of your body serve God, so that you will belong completely to him" (Romans 6:19 CEV).

No person is exempt from the curse of guilt and sin, but it is reassuring to know God made a provision: When we become a child of God we are set free from the bondage of sin. The Lord gives us the power to shed the shackles of habits and addictions to release us from that captivity. (See John 8:34-36).

God's Provision for Guilt

People remain stuck when they continue to rehash things they should have handled in a different way. It's time to use a spiritual "Drain-O" to clean out the pipes. There are two stages in the process. First, we pour in the spiritual cleansing agent—confessing our sin(s). Second, we express gratitude and thanksgiving for God's provision of Living Water which keeps guilt flushed out so it no longer poisons our thought-life. If we need to make restitution for any wrong-doing, we take care of that and then—let it go.

If Drain-O is left in the pipes in the sink, it can eat them up. In the same way, if guilt is stored in the mind, it eats away a healthy self-image.

You Choose the Path

When guilt enters the life of a person, we have the option of following one of two paths. Guilt and regret are usually experienced by Christians and sinners alike. The difference is how one chooses to deal with these two.

GUILT

REGRET

REMORSE	REPENTANCE
REPRESSION	RELEASE
CONDEMNATION	SANCTIFICATION

"Such (former) ages of ignorance God, it is true, ignored and allowed it to pass unnoticed; but now He charges all people everywhere to repent (to change their minds for the better and heartily to amend their ways, with abhorrence for their past sins" (Acts 17:30 AMP). We can't sow wild oats and hope they don't sprout and produce a bad crop. When crops turn out to be thorns and thistles, they must be removed from the field, lest their seeds reproduce a cursed crop, year after year.

"Where is the god who can compare with you— wiping the slate clean of guilt, turning a blind eye, a deaf ear, to the past sins of your purged and precious people? You don't nurse your anger and don't stay angry long, for mercy is your specialty. That's what you love most. And compassion is on its way to us. You'll stamp out our wrongdoing. You'll sink our sins to the bottom of the ocean" (Micah 7:18-20 MSG). What wondrous relief that the guilt that plagues the world can be unloaded. It is not just covered over or hidden. Blessed peace comes as this burden is released. Our records have been wiped clean as sins are confessed and we are set free.

MY BURDENS

I look back on yesterday—its load I cannot bear
Guilt, sin and failure confront me everywhere.

Hurts and grudges poison my past,
Clouds role in— dark shadows are cast.

Future dread floods over my heart.
Fear of failure tears me apart.

Will there be acceptance, will I find love?
So I am trapped, 'til I look above.

A small voice whispers sweet and clear—
"I am with you," is the message I hear.

"Come to me, I'll give you rest."
An open invitation as His honored guest.

He offers to rid me of my worrisome load.
He knows the journey; He's traveled this road.

This frees me to carry my cross for today
His strength lifts me up to go on my way.

He showers me with love, joy and peace—
I'm ready to travel—life holds a new lease.

Thank you, Father, you really do care.
I'll follow You forever and dwell with You there.

LLL

Lord, break any chains that bind me to my past sins and mistakes.

SCRIPTURES TO CONSIDER

James 5:16
James 4:7
Galatians 6:2
Romans 6:19
Psalms 32:1-6

QUESTIONS FOR DISCUSSION

1. Why do you believe God has us confess our sins? What happens when we do?

2. How does the enemy use guilt to immobilize us?

3. How can we depend on God's Truth instead of our feelings to accept His forgiveness?

4. Do you continue to think over and over of things you've done wrong?

5. Do you try to compensate for bad things you have done or failed to do? If so, How?

6. What might you do to help let go of the past?

21

FORGIVE TO BE FORGIVEN

By forgiving, we receive forgiveness

To know and experience the grace of God's forgiveness is, in a sense, like winning the lottery and receiving a huge unearned gift. But far better, it is the avenue by which our Father sends His unconditional love and mercy. It doesn't fit into our rational thinking. Many go to great lengths to explain to God and others why they don't deserve to be forgiven. They accept as fact an old expression, "I made my bed—therefore I must lie in it."

A Simple but Often Misunderstood Teaching

Perhaps one of the most misunderstood biblical concepts is that of forgiveness. It's hard to comprehend and extremely difficult to give or receive. Even those who know God can hardly fathom the divine blessing of this wondrous gift. It is sad to know there are those who attend church regularly who have no true understanding of the beautiful significance of forgiveness.

To refuse to accept God's provision and be set free is to reject a gift from God. We appoint ourselves as our own judge, to decide the penalty we're to pay for our sins. Then we sentence ourselves to a prison of our own making. This is audacious as well as sinful. When we face the worst that is in us, it's time to confess and ask the Lord to cleanse us. In doing this, we become marvelously cleansed—scrubbed, spit-and-polished, sinless, and shining inside and out.

We marvel at the depth of the meaning of the scripture which assures us, "Now to him who is able to do immeasurably more than all we ask or imagine, according to his power that is at work within us, to him be glory in the church and in Christ Jesus throughout all generations, forever and ever! Amen" (Ephesians 3:20-22 NIV).

God has chosen to love those who spit in His face and kick Him in the shins in a response to the beauty of His grace and the countless blessings He has sent. Millions still turn their backs on Him, use His name in vain and with a cocky attitude announce, "I don't need Him as a crutch."

Despite our arrogance, He continues to reach out to us. "God didn't go to all the trouble of sending His Son merely to point an accusing finger and tell us how bad we are. He came to help, to put the world right again. Anyone who trusts in Him is acquitted; anyone who refuses to trust Him has long since been under the death sentence without knowing it" (John 3:17-18 MSG).

Too often we wait until our world is crumbling and falling apart to decide to turn to God or turn against Him. When we hit rock bottom, it's time climb upon the altar of surrender and confess, "Okay, Lord, I can't do it. I need your answers and your help."

Pride fills us with ourselves so there's little or no room for God. Humility is the emptying self out to make room for Him to live in us. The Greek word that means "self-emptying" is *kenosis*.

Riches for Fool's Gold

When we bring our defiant hearts to God and humbly ask His forgiveness, He gives us His supernatural blessing of unconditional love and acceptance. If we fail to accept this grace and mercy, we're left on our own to be beaten and defeated as William Cullen Bryant expressed in his poem, *Thanatopsis:* ". . .like a quarry slave at night, scourged to his dungeon . . ."

There is great freedom in releasing the guilt of our past sins to the Lord. "Come to me, all you who are weary and burdened, and I will give you rest" (Matthew 11:28). *Thank You, Lord.*

The nitty-gritty of the matter comes if we hang onto self-sufficiency—"I can handle things myself." If we push God away, it's impossible for us to receive the benefit of the Father's forgiveness. To learn how to forgive is to acknowledge God's goodness.

In this astonishing way, we partake of His divine nature. The lack of forgiveness is an impenetrable dam that blocks the flow of love—between God and man, as well as between man and the rest of mankind.

Check the Price Tag on Forgiveness

The word forgiving encompasses the words *for giving.* "For God so loved the world that He *gave.* . . ." (John 3:16 KJV). God purchased the incredible gift of forgiveness by paying the exorbitant price of His Son.

This boggles my mind. How the Father must have struggled before making the decision to offer His only Son as a guilt offering for every despicable sin of the world! No wonder his countenance was so horrible with all these sins hanging on the cross with Him.

No doubt the Father braced himself and stood back as He watched wicked men sentence Jesus to the excruciating death on the cross. Do you suppose God turned His head when Jesus sobbed, "Why have You forsaken me?"

Forgiving Others

When the conduit or pipe of good fellowship between two people becomes clogged and the flow of love is shut off or reduced, it usually indicates we need a plunger to clean out feelings of unforgiveness. It likely involves repenting of resentment and bitterness. It sounds simple, and yet can be so difficult to admit we've held onto a bad attitude and withheld loving concern.

In a similar, but to a much lesser degree than God's offering His Son, it costs us when we forgive others. It requires us to give up our rights and allow our roots of bitterness and resentment to be ripped out. It may be akin to surgery that is performed without an anesthetic. The scalpel of God's truth is sharp as it slices into the heart of a problem.

This self-sacrifice may need to be repeated more than once. While kneeling in contrition by our bedside, we must resist Satan's counsel to justify our feelings of resentment and suggest reasons why we have a right to refuse to forgive.

Some offer conditional forgiveness or set probation terms. We may be tempted to decide that the other person should pay penance or we say, "I forgive, but I won't forget." Mulling it over, we're tempted to procrastinate or decide not to forgive at all. Some have an unforgiving attitude, "Hurt me once, shame on you—hurt me twice, shame on me."

"Don't hit back; discover the beauty in everyone. If you've got it in you, get along with everybody. Don't insist on getting even; that's not for you to do. 'I'll do the judging,' says God. 'I'll take care of it'" (Romans 12:17-19 MSG).

Forgiving Self

Forgiveness of self may be the most difficult type of forgiveness. We've likely learned that God forgives and we even understand we're to forgive others. However, we often continue to pack around a load of shame because we reason there's no excuse for the way we've messed up our lives.

The Word tells us that the price for all unworthiness has been paid for, so how do we have the audacity to think we're an exception? We must never underestimate the power of the blood of Jesus.

Asking Other's Forgiveness

While it may be a struggle to confess our sins to God, it's harder to admit our sins to those we've offended. It's a challenge to ask their forgiveness. Our human nature makes us feel awkward when we stand before someone we've wronged. We may feel like a penny waiting for change. "I apologize, please forgive me for I was wrong" sticks in our craw because we're so determined to always be right.

In order to deal with sin that's hidden in the dark, it must be exposed to the light. Confession brings our sins to the surface where God wipes our slate clean. "Make this your common practice: Confess your sins to each other and pray for each other so that you can live together whole and healed. The prayer of a person living right with God is something powerful to be reckoned with" (James 5:16 MSG).

Sins are never forgiven by confessing someone *else's* sin. It's brutal and sinful when we gossip and whisper about other's failures.

"Make a clean break with all cutting, backbiting, and profane talk. Be gentle with one another, sensitive. Forgive one another as quickly and thoroughly as God in Christ forgave you" (Ephesians 4:31-32 MSG).

It's ridiculous to pretend other's sins should be written in concrete, while our own sins are written in sand, to be washed away by the tide.

Total Forgiveness

Feeble excuses are evidence we've not dealt with our sins. It's like using a dirty eraser in an attempt to remove scribbled marks on a paper. There are still dirty smudges as evidence of mistakes that were there. Only God's mandate will wash away our sins until there's no evidence of anything ever written on our record.

Since forgiveness is bathed in God's grace, past incidents may be recalled, but they'll no longer harass us with shame and guilt. His grace suctions out all the negative emotions surrounding a bad memory.

This was experienced by the Apostle Paul: "Brothers, I do not consider myself yet to have taken hold of it. But one thing I do: Forgetting what is behind and straining towards what is ahead, I press on towards the goal to win the prize for which God has called me heavenwards in Christ Jesus" (Philippians 3:13-14 NIV). God has given us a healthy method to further remove evidence of negative emotions that accompany unforgiveness.

Have the Courage to Say, "I Was Wrong"

When we admit we've done wrong, we must guard against adding a postscript of excuses, attempting to justify why we did what we did or said what we said. Once I was betrayed and treated with humiliation and disrespect. Months later, I confronted the one who hurt me. "You've never asked for forgiveness."

The person's response was flippant. "If my actions don't express that I'm sorry, then it won't do any good to ask for forgiveness."

His excuse was flimsy—it didn't hold water or meet God's requirement. His answer might well be compared to standing on a wet soap box to defend his actions. It expressed little or no regret for the pain he'd caused. In my mind, his reasoning crumpled and fell flat.

"If we claim we are not guilty of sin, we're only fooling ourselves. A claim like that is errant nonsense. On the other hand, if we admit our sins—make a clean breast of them—He won't let us down; He'll be true to himself. He'll forgive our sins and purge us of all wrongdoing. If we claim that we've never sinned, we out-and-out contradict God—make a liar out of Him (1 John 1:8-10 MSG).

The Power of Confession

It isn't sufficient to simply confess to God. This still allows us to conceal our weaknesses from another human being. We must be humble enough to "come clean" about our shortcomings to others. "Therefore confess your sins to each other and pray for each other so that you may be healed" (James 5:16 NIV).

In the midst of a retreat, when people were examining their inner motives, my son, Paul, asked a pastor's wife if she wanted to share anything with the group. She hesitated a moment, pressed her lips together and said, "Yes, I'm ready to confess something I've been hiding for a long time."

She dropped her head and spoke in a quieter tone. "I shoplifted for years. Ultimately, I was caught and taken to jail, where I had to spend the night. Our family was so humiliated we moved from that community. Though I stopped shoplifting, I've never been able to forgive myself."

Paul questioned her further. "What did you just do?"

She looked up and smiled. "I've chosen to do the very thing I feared would happen—for others to know the terrible thing I'd done." She took a long breath and released it slowly. "Since I chose to tell this group, I no longer face the fear of others discovering that humiliating experience." Her eyes swept around the room to see how each member of the group responded to what she'd confessed. "I'm finally ready to forgive myself and go on." The group reached out to her in tender compassion and encouragement. The heavy load was lifted from her soul.

Father, I don't understand why it is so difficult for us to confess our sins to one another. Is it because we don't want others to think less of us? Forgive us when our pride stands in the way of confessing and holds us hostage by those hidden sins.

SCRIPTURES TO CONSIDER

Proverbs 18:12
Romans 1:29–31
1 Corinthians 6:9–11
1 Thessalonians 4:9

QUESTIONS FOR DISCUSSION

1. Why is it so difficult to forgive yourself when God has prom-
    ised His forgiveness?

2. Describe what you think heaven will be like.

3. Why do so many of us wait until the worlds close to total
    turmoil before we turn to God?

4. How has the devil deceived many by convincing them that
    God is a crutch?

5. Why is it so common for people to attempt things without
    consulting God or asking for His help?

22

PAID IN FULL

I'm so glad I don't get what I deserve

There's an old saying, "beside every new grave there is someone who believes he's somewhat responsible for the person's death." It's sad when one pounds himself with accusations. "If I had only . . ." or "if I hadn't . . ." Though it is reasonable to accept some responsibility in the way people's lives turn out—or end, still each individual has a choice as to what they do with their own circumstances.

When we make mistakes, we have several choices: (1) Accept or excuse ourselves for what happened, (2) distract ourselves and refuse to look at the wrong, (3) punish ourselves with guilt, or (4) repent and then watch God pick up the pieces to put us back together properly.

Most parents are aware of mistakes they've made in child rearing. There was a time when I told God, "I wish I could start over again," but I realized I'd probably make a whole new set of mistakes.

Penalties

When three-year-old Bobby hit his little sister, his mother sent him out to find a switch that would sting his legs. She scolded, "I don't want you to ever forget you need to be nice to your baby sister." After a period of time she called, "Bobby, get yourself in here! What's taking you so long?"

Bobby appeared at the door with a clenched fist and held it up to his mother and whimpered, "I couldn't find a switch, but here is a wock you can fro at me." Perhaps the little guy felt that if his mom hit him with a rock, it would make her feel better. He missed the point—just as we sometimes do when we fail to understand that

God disciplines those He loves because He wants to encourage His children to live their very best.

Capital Punishment

Some who've been traumatized by the murder of a family member have thought that if they could watch the perpetrator die, it would relieve much of the pain caused by their horrific loss. This seldom happens. Only God, our Righteous Judge, is qualified to mete out appropriate punishment for sin, along with the provision to heal the broken-hearted.

In an unimaginable act of love, our Father chose to offer His only Son to bear the consequences of sins which would have condemned us. We're given the blessed privilege to scoop up our sins and lay them at the foot of the cross where Jesus picks them up and clutches them close to His heart until they evaporate. We seldom forget our sins, but our Father forgives and forgets the moment we confess.

A prison warden told of witnessing a man sentenced to death. There, in the gallery above the scene of the execution, were two small rooms facing the criminal. One contained the family of the criminal, and the other, the loved ones of the victim.

The murderer was ushered in and charged to lie down on the table. The warden's heart pounded as he stood near the head of the criminal, facing the two families. When he adjusted his glasses, it was a signal for the deadly serum to be injected.

As he prepared for the procedure, he looked up and his heart ached as he watched the mother of the sentenced criminal weeping as she leaned her head against the wall. In the room next to her, the mother of the victim wept—her head resting on the opposite side of the same wall—only a few inches separated their heads. The loss of life proved to be heart-rending to both families.

Do We Value Human Life?

When I taught in a maximum security prison, I walked into my classroom and overheard two prisoners talking. One spoke in a sarcastic way to another standing nearby. "I thought you said you were a Christian."

The other answered indignantly. "I *am* a Christian."

"Then what are you in here for?"

"I *just* killed a guy."

On another occasion, I went to the office to report a student who constantly grumbled and complained. The principal told me to go back and warn him once. If he failed to change his attitude, he would be permanently removed from the classroom and sent to work in the fields. A trustee who worked in the office got up and followed me down the hall. "Who is he?"

I looked at him questioning, "Why do you want to know?"

He snapped his fingers, "I'll kill him tonight, like this. No one will ever know what happened."

Cold chills played tag up and down my spine. He was serious. He was in prison for life, and what happened to him (or others) appeared to be of little significance.

The general concept is that people must be punished in a way that's appropriate for their crimes. Others contend it isn't politically correct to treat criminals in any way that would be harsh, regardless of what they've done. The brutality of some violent acts makes one wonder whether their punishment could possibly be a deterrent to crime. But then again, why does God choose to not treat us in the way our sins deserve? His unmerited favor of grace receives us, relieves us and frees us when we humbly accept His unconditional love.

Self-condemned Martyrs

A person with an over-active guilt-complex continues to kick himself and figuratively beats himself over the head for his offenses. He responds as if he owes a debt with compound interest that can never be paid—regardless of how long he strives or suffers.

A self-imposed martyr brings no glory to God when the person assumes the responsibility of paying for his own sins. We slap our Heavenly Father in the face when we refuse to accept Jesus' death as a sufficient penalty to pay for sin.

How blessed we are when we understand, "Those who enter into Christ's being-here-for-us no longer have to live under a continuous low-lying black cloud. A new power is in operation. The spirit of the life in Christ, like a strong wind, has magnificently cleared the air, freeing you from the fated lifetime of brutal tyranny at the hands of sin and death" (Romans 8:1-2 MSG).

Self-punishment

A photo of a man from India portrayed this misunderstood concept in a vivid way. His torso was covered with fishhooks that punctured his flesh. Each fishhook had a lead weight attached to the end of it. The weights dangled as he walked and inflicted excruciating pain. He did this because he thought he deserved ongoing punishment for his wrong-doings. It focused on sins, rather than redemption.

Whether it is from guilt or self-hatred, an increasing number of people continue to cut themselves. The instigator of this self-mutilation is Satan himself, whose very purpose is to rob, kill and destroy.

One lady confessed she had no explanation for times she'd find herself in the bathroom or digging through a drawer in the kitchen, looking for a knife or a razor blade to cut herself. Even when a glass was accidently broken, the enemy stood nearby and whispered, "Slash your wrists and get it over with."

No Substitutes for Confession and Repentance

When I was five, I stole a nickel I'd found at the home of a friend. I took it home and hid it so well I never was able to spend it. Over the years, I gave my friend gifts and bought her candy, but never confessed I'd stolen the money. I paid her back many times over for the nickel I'd stolen, but that did not atone for what I'd done. Nor did it remove any guilt feelings. It was a feeble attempt to offset the bad by trying to compensate with good.

We receive God's declaration of "not guilty" through confession. This calls for us to respond in wholehearted praise for the One whose mercy takes us under His wing. He seals our relationship with Him with the beautiful word "atone." This word breaks down to "at one" with the Father. How beautiful that a person can be forgiven without suffering. On the other hand, some continue to suffer because they fail to accept God's forgiveness.

Redeemed

How humbled we are when we review what God has done for us. If it were not for His unmerited favor, we'd be condemned to live under the curse of the sins we've committed. But thank God, Jesus took away that curse. He received the death penalty we deserved.

"Christ redeemed us from that self-defeating, cursed life by absorbing it completely into himself. Do you remember the Scripture that says, 'Cursed is everyone who hangs on a tree'" (Galatians 3:13 CEV)?

There is no better way to grasp the impact of what Jesus did for us than the way Eugene Peterson expressed in the Message: "Call out to God for help and He helps—He's a good Father that way. But don't forget, He's also a responsible Father, and won't let you get by with sloppy living. Your life is a journey you must travel with a deep consciousness of God. It cost God plenty to get you out of that dead-end, empty-headed life you grew up in. He paid with Christ's sacred blood, you know. . ." (1 Peter 1:17-18 MSG).

If there had been another way the Father's unconditional love could have been expressed, He no doubt would've never allowed His Son to die on a cross. In our limited understanding, we can't grasp how He could stand back and watch enemies torture His only child as payment for the sins of the world—including mine. How sad for us to go for long periods of time without expressing our gratitude for this sacrifice.

How wonderful when we accept God's promise: " . . .being confident of this, that He who began a good work in you will carry it on to completion until the day of Christ Jesus" (Philippians 1:6 NIV). Thank you, Almighty God, we have been redeemed!

Let my thankfulness explode in praise. Prompt me to express again and again my overwhelming gratitude for loving me enough to pay the ultimate price that I might be forever free from the guilt of sin.

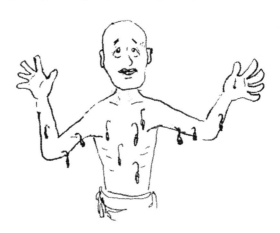

SCRIPTURES TO CONSIDER

Romans 8:1-2
Galatians 3:13
1 Peter 1:17-18
Philippians 1:6

QUESTIONS FOR DISCUSSION

1. The thoughts that come to mind when I first feel guilt is. . .

2. Are there still things you feel the need to forgive yourself for? What can you do?

3. God gives us the authority to resist Satan when he continues to harass us about the things we've done wrong. How are we to resist him? (See James 4:7)

4. How can you be confident God has forgiven you for the sins you've confessed?

5. Is there anything you need to make retribution (pay someone back for wrong)—or have you already taken care of this?

6. What one thing would you do differently if you could live your life over?

SECTION VII
INTERPERSONAL
RELATIONSHIPS

23

EMPATHY

Don't feel for me, feel with me

In order to have empathy—to be able to feel with someone, we must take time to listen and carefully observe people, to make sure we know where they're coming from. When people have similar backgrounds, it is easier to relate to them. I struggled with an identity problem when I taught in a maximum security prison. I asked for God's wisdom to understand what it would be like to be locked in a cell day and night as these prisoners were.

Men who were incarcerated in the prison sometimes cocked their heads and sized me up with a look of suspicion, "You act like you really like us."

I'd grin with a bit of a tease in my voice and respond, "Oh, I do like you. Others may think you're not worth a plugged nickel, but I think you're pretty neat." I'd pause a moment while they chuckled and then continue, "Have you ever had anyone else who cared for you?"

Their smiles vanished and a look of solemn regret replaced them.

More than one commented, "I don't think I've ever had anyone who cared whether I lived or died." They considered themselves worthless— therefore unlovable and unwanted.

John Donne wrote "no man is an island." But if the basic need of love and empathy has failed to wash over our shores and water our souls, we'd certainly live in a lonely place, in isolation. If we've not received love or had those who attempted to understand us, how can we know how to show genuine concern for others?

Empathy and understanding are a natural outgrowth of love. The word is often used in an ambiguous way, ranging from our Father's love to a vulgar or cheap expression. Perhaps we could make an acronym of **L**iking **O**thers **V**ery **E**nthusiastically. In a blessed way, love tends to overlook flaws and to search for virtues that can be sanctioned by encouragement.

Empathy

One night I heard my eight-year-old son, Rick, crying in his room. I knelt by his bedside and asked him to tell me what was wrong. It took a while to persuade him to open up, but he finally admitted, "Mom, I was looking in a magazine and saw a picture of starving children, and I can't take them any food to eat." My heart was touched by his loving concern. I wish I'd thought to tell him we'd get in contact with an agency that sent food to hungry children, but I didn't. I comforted him as best I could and left him grieving with his compassionate heart.

My niece, Celia, admired a beautiful winter coat in a store when she and her mom were shopping. Her mother went back later and bought the coat for her Christmas present. It would replace one Celia had purchased at a Goodwill Store and patched at the elbows. Her mother beamed with excitement as she watched her open the gift. Her heart glowed as Celia put the coat on and snuggled in its cozy warmth.

Back at college, in the dormitory, Celia was in another girl's room who bemoaned, "I need to go to class but I wish I had a coat. It's already beginning to snow." Celia went back to her room and pulled out her brand new coat, returned to her classmate's room and handed it to her. "Here, take this, I have another one." What a wonderful example of empathy, wrapped in a warm coat of compassion and love. When Celia's mother found out what she'd done, she fussed at her. "I guess we'll have to go and buy you another coat."

Celia shook her head, "Mom, you just don't get it."

Empathy cloaked in understanding comes close to living in another's skin. If we can achieve this, our thought patterns line up with their hurts and pain. These are not only felt in vicarious ways, but almost with the same intensity as the one going through the actual experience.

As empathy is stirred from deep within the heart, it builds a bridge that allows us to cross over to walk side-by-side with another. However, we honor them when we wait until they give us permission to come alongside.

Someone Please Talk to Me

Even though I live alone, I enjoy the benefit of having someone who empathizes with me. I talk to the Lord as if He were present in the room, sitting in a chair next to me. He made me, so I'm confident He understands me. I seldom feel lonely or uncared for. Even so, I still appreciate having others around that have flesh and blood.

Since we've experienced a mass exodus from rural areas to urban complexes, close relationships have often been replaced with "social networking." Every year, as technology progresses, we experience less and less meaningful eyeball-to-eyeball or face-to-face contact. Our society has become *so* depersonalized.

Vulnerable people are sucked into dangerous relationships through chat rooms. It's easy to be misled when one yearns for someone who will come on board as an answer to their dreams. Deception plays a part when someone comes across with what they think sounds good and makes them appear as a "knight in shining armor."

My level of frustration rises when I make a call, then have it short-circuited by a recorded message, followed by a series of "punch one . . .punch two . . ." My teeth clench tighter waiting for the option I need. When I fail to hear the appropriate response, the recording continues, "Push seven to repeat this message." Empathy is never expressed in a pre-recorded message. There's no way a depersonal-ized mechanical device can understand my specific problem.

But when a live voice replaces the prerecorded message, it frequently produces further frustration because the person on the line has such an accent, I can't understand them.

Will Someone Listen to Me?

In our gadget-prone era, families are spending less and less time together. "Busy" may sound impressive to us and may be mistaken as an indication of our importance. Busyness contributes to our becoming overly involved, which isn't always wise. We act in much the same way as the Mad Hatter, who along with the flustered rabbit lamented, "I'm late, I'm late, for a very important date."

The advice column, "Dear Abby" was written to respond to "Joe Blow's" concerns. This was further characterized by Charles Shultz in his cartoon *Peanuts* when he featured Lucy sitting at her little psychiatrist's booth, offering her service for five cents. She was accustomed to offering advice, and this project had an added bonus of being able to charge for it.

The suicide prevention hotlines attend to the critical cry from people who are grasping for a straw to hang onto. In cities, these hotlines receive call after call, day after day and night after night. Desperate and hurting people are searching for someone who understands and will give them a reason to live.

How reassuring it is to know we can call on God. He is always available. He not only listens, but He has great empathy and wants us to include Him in every struggle we face.

Fake It Till You Make It

We had a "walking sprinkler" that straddled a water hose. Water pressure caused the gears to turn and move it forward with a powerful torque. One afternoon, I turned off the water in order to move the sprinkler to another location.

I must have responded too quickly because when I stuck my foot out to stop the whirling motion of the sprinkler, the metal arm whacked my ankle. I screeched and hobbled into the house to find my husband, so I could wail to him about my accident. He glanced at the injured ankle briefly and mumbled, "Well, you need to learn to be more careful." With that, he walked out the door to go to the store.

When he returned a while later, I was lying on the couch, still moaning about my painful experience. He took a closer look. Shock swept across his face when he saw how badly my ankle and foot were discolored—black, blue and a tinge of green. It looked awful. "We have to get you to the doctor and have it X-rayed," he said. "Your ankle may be broken."

I played the martyr. "No, I'll be okay, just let me lay here awhile." He apologized for his previous lack of concern and made me comfortable with pillows and an ice pack. He brought me a Dr. Pepper to drink. After several minutes of sympathy and apologies, I piped, "Okay, that's enough, I can go wash it off now."

I used the situation as an opportunity to be creative in order to get my needs met. My conniving mind prompted me to take my water colors and do a masterful job of decorating my foot and ankle. Carey's mouth dropped open as he gasped. I'd faked him out. While he was still searching for words, I warned, "The next time I hurt myself, you'd better show me the love and sympathy I need."

Understanding Our Children

Parents should make it a habit to pray before they preach. When parents and children don't take time to share their problems, the relationship shrivels until it is dry and parched. There's a possibility it will shrink until it's lost all its value.

One absent father tried to confront his son about his behavior and the teenage son snapped, "Why should I listen to you—you've never been here to listen to me." The harsh words were convicting, but the father got angry and his lack of understanding drove them further apart.

When my oldest son, Rick, was little he kept interrupting his prayers to talk about other things. I insisted he finish talking to God before he talked to me. One night when he prayed, he mentioned everyone, including his dog, and then added, "And dear God, don't let the spiders get us—and tell Mom there's one a'crawlin down the wall behind her back."

If we expect God to understand us, we must spend quality time searching for what He wants for our lives. How comforting to know we can give Him all our worries and cares, because He's always thinking about us and understands our every concern. Even when I don't feel His presence, I know our Father is true to His promises and is ever present. No one ever needs to bemoan, "Is there anyone out there?"

We have our needs for empathy supplied because God cares, Jesus understands and the Holy Spirit comforts and guides. Sometimes in difficult situations, I think I hear Jesus whisper, "I understand."

"Shout for joy, you heavens; rejoice, you earth; burst into song, you mountains! For the Lord comforts his people and will have compassion on his afflicted ones" (Isaiah 49:13 NIV).

The Human Reflection

As a part of the family of God, we're to empathize with one another. "Laugh with happy friends when they're happy; share tears when they're down" (Romans 12:15 MSG). It's difficult for me to be kneeling beside someone or flat on my face and remain prideful. The position I'm in helps me maintain empathy and a caring attitude in dealing with others. If I'm wrapped up in myself, I'm a small package that isn't an appropriate gift for anyone.

Empathy is cultivated as we involve ourselves in another person's feelings, problems and heartaches. God intended for at least a portion of our needs to be met through friendship. We nurture bonding when we bear one another's burdens. We were meant to share each other's troubles and problems. We not only have God, but other members of the body of Christ standing by.

When we continue to stuff our feelings, they become a heavy load because we assume we're to carry these burdens alone. However, if we share our hurts and pains, we distribute them. They aren't too burdensome when we have others volunteering to help us carry them.

We are admonished to comfort those who are frightened and take tender care of those who are weak. "Praise be to the God and Father of our Lord Jesus Christ, the Father of compassion and the God of all comfort, who comforts us in all our troubles, so that we can comfort those in any trouble with the comfort we ourselves receive from God" (2 Corinthians 1:3-4 NIV). This is a biblical example that clearly defines empathy.

Have you ever held hands in a circle and your hands begin to pulsate as if in sync with those standing next to you? The connection is strong and unity solid when we are one in the Spirit. The Trinity gives us love, understanding and acceptance. The Godhead feels our hurts and shares our joy. This team empowers us with strength when we are weak and it also gives us guidance when we've lost our way. In Him we are complete, our needs supplied, and our hopes and dreams are actualized.

Thank you Lord. You rule over the whole Universe, yet You're always available and approachable. You encourage me when life seems to be falling apart. I don't have to stand in line or make an appointment. You listen with rapt attention and understanding, as if I were Your only child.

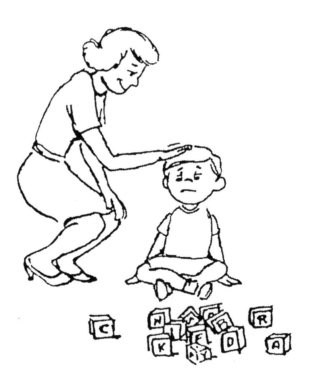

SCRIPTURES TO CONSIDER

Luke 18:1-8
Romans 8:26-28
Galatians 6:2-4
1 Thessalonians 5:11, 14, 15
Hebrews 2:18, 4:14-15

QUESTIONS FOR DISCUSSION

1. My primary source of meeting my need for love-empathy is . . . (A person or something you do.)

2. The ways I can reach out to others with love-empathy is by . . .

3. Name a relationship you think would be improved if you understood the person better?

4. What would be a step you could take to help that relationship?

5. Have you avoided being around an individual or group that you have difficulty understanding?

6. What could your family do to help you bond better?

24

THE DYNAMIC POWER OF WORDS

The words we speak have the power of life or death

Be careful! The tongue resides in a wet and slippery place. Therefore, it's easy for words to slither out, causing us to fall flat on our faces in mud puddles of regret. "This is scary. You can tame a tiger, but you can't tame a tongue—it has never been done. The tongue runs wild, a wanton killer" (James 3:7 MSG).

The power of God's spoken Word is impressive, beyond imagination. Our Creator spoke the heavens and the earth into existence with His Word. Every cell, every atom and molecule stands at attention, ready to do the Lord's bidding.

This kind of obedience is evident throughout the entire universe—regardless of how large or small—from the tiniest living organism to the mightiest mountain and galaxies beyond the scope of our most powerful telescopes. Most things start small.

The world was whispered into existence with a Word, not a *big bang*.

Man Wasn't Spoken into Existence

It is intriguing that God created everything with a Word—with the exception of man. With His hands, He molded him from the dust of the earth—then breathed His own breath of life into him. The body was made from the earth but the spirit came alive with the breath of God. When we were in the womb, it wasn't a matter of artificial respiration but by supernatural aspiration that we were ushered into life. "Then the Lord God formed man of the dust of the ground, and breathed into his nostrils the breath or spirit of life; and man became a living being" (Genesis 2:7 AMP).

Though we are mortal, we're brought to life in order for us to become immortal.

In an opposite way, we may use *our* words to make dirt out of another's reputation. This was *not* God's purpose. His breath was given as our commission to breathe life and encouragement into others. "Watch the way you talk. Let nothing foul or dirty come out of your mouth. Say only what helps, each word a gift" (Ephesians 4:29 MSG).

Since man was made in the image of God, He fashioned him as His "hands on" crowning work. Creation was spoken into existence—a product of God's creativity of beauty and enjoyment. But man's sculptured purpose was to become a companion of God—closely akin to His Divine nature.

Words Build up or Destroy

Truth is the dance of words that waltzes into our heart and dispenses any clanging confusion. People send messages that either encourage or discourage us. It's important for us to learn to make sure our perception lines up with the song God sings over us.

A very influential millionaire wept as he told the group at a retreat that he'd never been able to please his biological father. He'd never received encouragement from the man who should have been his strongest supporter. "My dad cut me down by magnifying every mistake I made and focused on anything he could think of that was wrong with me. He never stopped telling me,' "You could have done better."'

People may try to justify what they say by commenting, "I didn't mean it—I was just teasing." Even if a person doesn't mean what he says—what he says can be downright *mean*. How grateful we are that our heavenly Father doesn't treat us this way. Even when we fall on our face, He is there to help us up to whisper deep in our spirit, "you can make it."

But it's sobering to know a day is coming when we'll give an account of every idle word we speak. "But I tell you that men will have to give account on the Day of Judgment for every careless word they have spoken" (Matthew 12:36 NLT).

Noise Levels and Silence

Think of the airways and the jillions of sounds that are carried across continents through television, radio, telephones and honking horns. Will the vast universe one day become saturated with unrelenting noise? If all sounds were combined, wouldn't the whole universe explode?

Some of the most powerful occurrences in nature are accompanied by sound. Thunder is the companion of lightning. The volcano erupts with deafening rumblings and roaring. Waves crash against the rocks. The wind howls and we're told the sound of a tornado is similar to a freight train barreling through. Even man expresses his exuberance with a shout. Since all sounds are forever in the atmosphere, it's no wonder Satan continues to recycle accusing words to condemn us.

It's interesting that the Bible tells us that nature expresses itself with different expressions of praise: The hills sing, the trees clap their hands, the rocks cry out. Though tradition tells us that silence is golden, Solomon said, "A word aptly spoken is like apples of gold in settings of silver" (Proverbs 25:11 NIV).

Some phenomena speak powerfully by their presence, without a sound. Early morning sun bursts over the horizon without a whisper, in spite of all its heat and energy. In silence, a cherry tree explodes with blossoms. Though a mother may scream when she's giving birth, the baby slips quietly through the birth canal before announcing his arrival with a wail.

It is so important for a person not only to say the right thing, but timing is also extremely important. What may be appropriate to say at one time could be rude and inappropriate at another time. "Words from a wise man's mouth are gracious, but a fool is consumed by his own lips" (Ecclesiastes 10:12 NIV).

Flattery and Exaggeration

Flattery is like putting a beautiful glaze on a piece of cracked pottery. It may conceal the flaws underneath, but it doesn't hold the water of honesty or integrity. Flattery is so sticky sweet it's almost nauseous.

Flattery makes me feel as if I've been buttered up before being slipped under the broiler to cook my goose.

A person may grovel on his face in bootlicking flattery, but prayer is a far better choice for that position. Flattering words don't mean anything to God—He listens to our heart. If I begin to use flowery words in prayer, I can almost hear Him say, "Get real."

We're tempted to embellish our stories to make them sound more sensational. My husband, Carey, used to challenge me in a joking way, "I've told you a million times not to exaggerate."

When my brother, Sam, was five, my older sister swatted him for slamming my fingers in the door. He looked up to her with gritted teeth, "When I grow up, I'll get as big as a windmill and "whup you." My brother grew up and even grew tall, but he never beat her up.

Misunderstanding

Many of us played the "gossip" game as children when we sat in a circle and the leader whispered a phrase in the ear of the one sitting beside her. This person whispered the message to the next until the circle was completed. The last person was asked to share what she heard. The participants usually burst out with peals of laughter, because what the last one understood had little or nothing to do with the original message. Sadly, this is also true when gossip spreads—getting further and further from the truth.

We're guilty at times of speaking before we think. It would be nice if those comments went in one ear and out the other, but unfortunately, that's not always the case. We need to repeat the prayer King David prayed, "Let the words of my mouth, and the meditation of my heart, be acceptable in thy sight, O Lord, my strength, and my Redeemer" (Psalms 19:14 KJV). Our words are to come from a pure heart.

God's Name is Holy

It is not uncommon for many to use the name of God or Jesus *in vain.* "No using the name of GOD, your God, in curses or silly banter; GOD won't put up with the irreverent use of his name" (Exodus 20:7 MSG). Even some Christians are guilty of commenting, "Oh God," as a casual insert, with little or no reverence attached.

How will we stand before God and confess our disrespect? Do we forget that we'll give an account for tossing our Father's name around as if it were something to play with? As a part of the Ten

Commandments, casual use of God's name is in total disregard for His holiness.

Words in Action

God's Word is irrevocable Truth. We'd do well to make sure our words are true. There's a derogative expression for those who "talk out of both sides of their mouths."

"With our tongues we bless God our Father; with the same tongue we curse the very men and women He made in His image. Curses and blessings out of the same mouth. My friends, this can't go on. . ." (James 3:9-10 MSG).

It's deceptive when a person says all the right things, yet doesn't walk out the truth he claims to believe. Our true beliefs are reflected in how we live. We use the expression of someone "talking a good game," or we refer to a person speaking with "tongue in cheek." It gives us some reservations concerning what they say.

"Don't bad-mouth each other, friends, it's God's Word, His Message, His Royal Rule, that takes a beating in that kind of talk. You're supposed to be honoring the Message, not writing graffiti all over it" (James 4:11 MSG).

Dear heavenly Father, keep us plugged to Holy Spirit power in order to live a dynamic and overcoming life.

SCRIPTURES TO CONSIDER

James 3:7-10
Matthew 12:36]
Proverbs 25:11
Psalms 19:14
2 Corinthians 1:7
James 4:11

QUESTIONS FOR DISCUSSION

1. Can you remember when you said something that was inappropriate? Explain.

2. Have you ever been deeply hurt by what someone said about you? Talk about it

3. Were there things your parents said about you that influenced your life?

4. Is sarcasm ever helpful? Explain.

5. Has anyone ever greatly influenced you with words of encouragement? Explain.

6. How does it make you feel when someone flatters you?

25

WHAT WERE YOU SAYING?

Some speak softly but carry a big stick

Communication provides a way to offer and receive ideas, thoughts and opinions. It is the bridge of understanding that either gives us the rite of passage into another's life or we burn that bridge behind us, separating us from an enhanced relationship. Without proper interaction, we leave others as islands in a sea of humanity—without access, disconnected and alone.

Lack of good communication creates a wall of misunderstanding that is often too high to scale or jump over. That wall may be as solid and impenetrable as if it were made of stone.

Perhaps the best illustration of the way messages are conveyed is thinking of them as being funneled through a pipe. The value of a pipe is often measured in how much liquid can flow through. Communication is the pipe through which blessings or curses are exchanged—whether it is refreshing water or sewage.

However, if this exchange is limited to a small soda straw, it restricts conversations to a tiny stream which is easily crimped to stop the flow altogether. But a large pipe or conduit is capable of handling a large volume of ideas, thoughts and dreams—flowing from deep wells of our innermost being.

It Takes Time and Effort

Relationships are enhanced by a two-way exchange of ideas. I get in trouble if I don't make an effort to listen to others with rapt attention and discernment. It's only under close observation that one hears the heartbeat of another and discovers deeper meaning underneath what they say. Opinions are often inaccurate and distorted as a result of poor communication. If our pipes are clogged, mental pictures get out of focus.

When we determine to both talk, then listen, we'll capture a true picture of where another person is coming from. If there are disagreements, they can be worked through—or at least we can come to an understanding of those differences. However, if two people don't communicate well, the smallest problem can muddy the relationship and cut off the clean flow of blessings available through the friendship.

Gaps

Often a poor relationship between parents and their children is not only because of a generation gap, it's also compounded by a communication gap. When hormones are flowing, a teen may be frustrated and have difficulty adapting to those changes. His moods swing from one extreme to another. He can be jubilant, radical or defiant. Clashes seem inevitable. There are times when neither parent nor teen has any earthly idea where the other is coming from. And the sad truth is, they may get to a point where they don't care.

Many have a problem conversing as they would like with those of any age. A humorous saying is garbled: "I know that you understand what you think I said. However, I'm not sure that you realize that what I think you heard is not what I meant."

Non-Verbal Communication

Communication is both an intellectual and an emotional process. Words come across with facts and ideas, but body language offers greater depth behind the words themselves. Through non-spoken language, we can become more in tune with another's feelings. Close observation detects tension in a person's body, strains or quivers in their voice that reveal a more accurate story. Discernment notes expressions in eyes or fidgety hands. We listen to the words a person speaks as well as we pick up on the deeper message the body sends. Truth often crouches behind the spoken word. We hear the expression, "I can't hear what you're saying, because your actions speak louder than your words."

When emotional levels are at their peak, effective communication is often at its lowest. Overwhelming situations leave us speechless. We're likely to exaggerate when our emotions are in charge. If a person who is speaking is someone we love, we may justify or make excuses for inappropriate things they say. If, on the other hand, we're speaking with someone we don't care for, we may twist their message so that what we remember is negative, even degrading. We have a tendency to reinforce the opinion we already have of a person by "tweaking" the way we interpret what they say.

Remember, the enemy takes every opportunity to distort what we intend to convey. Severed relationships can be brought about from slight misunderstandings. We may alter other's input to fit opinions we've already formed, losing the real intent of their message. This is most obvious in politics when bits and pieces of a speech are taken out of context to purposely make the speaker appear ignorant or incompetent.

A surprisingly large percentage of our communication is nonverbal. Joy, sadness, fear, surprise, disgust, boredom, love and even disbelief can be conveyed through messages our bodies send. This body language is often a mirror of our heart. A raised eyebrow, a shrug of the shoulders, a wink of an eye, shaking or nodding the head or a clenched fist are dead give-a-ways. Such gestures send powerful messages.

My mother was modest and quiet, as well as a disciplined and controlled woman. Sometimes, the only way I could tell she was irritated was when I observed her drumming her fingers on the arm rest of her chair. This would be my clue to back off if I happened to be in the midst of forcing an issue.

Other Communication Problems

Since it is somewhat difficult to express our feelings, we may convey messages we'd rather not send. Keep this in mind when listening to others. We should guard against picking and choosing what we want to remember and be cautious about saying things we'd like others to forget.

Most people pick up on my true feelings. My attitudes seem to surface when I think I have them concealed. Too often people "read me" clear across the room by the way I act or look. If I'm upset, they detect my uneasiness. If I am happy, I almost glow. There would be no room for me at a poker table, because I could never maintain a "poker face."

One day when my niece and I were about to leave on a trip, drizzling rain darkened the day. The weather had turned cool. I started the car engine and then put the car in park. "I think I'll run back in and get a light jacket." When I returned, Laura asked, "Where's the life jacket?" We almost fell out of the car laughing when we realized she'd misunderstood me. She countered with, "Well, I knew it was raining, but I didn't anticipate we'd run into a flood."

This illustration is funny, yet when our communication skills fail, a person may be so misunderstood by another that it destroys their relationship. Voice inflections are also important. A person can say, "You smell *sweet*," yet change the entire meaning by expressing it, "You *smell*, sweet."

In other countries, words have different meanings. This is also true of gestures. Missionaries going to foreign fields have to be alert and not send wrong messages. Without meaning to, they may create a problem among the nationals.

Words have also changed meanings over the years. The word "gay" had a very different meaning when I was a child. We called flip-flops "thongs." I need to be careful how I use words that have different meanings now.

Debates and Arguments

Some people seem to delight in taking opposite positions and become adamant about their opinions. They make themselves a committee of one to either be a nonconformist or the devil's advocate. In junior high, my youngest son constantly picked arguments with me. Finally, his older sister, Kathy, pulled me aside. "Mom, don't you see what he's doing? He just likes to see you get riled up and irritated. If you won't allow yourself to get sucked into an argument, he'll probably stop."

I braced myself for the next time he attempted to bait me. I voiced my opinion and he made a conflicting statement. I ignored it. He responded with some outrageous comeback. I continued to prepare supper and paid no attention to him. Finally, he blurted, "How can we talk if you won't say anything?"

Responsibility to Speak Up

One of the weaknesses in the body of Christ is to see a fellow Christian doing something wrong, yet fail to address the problem. Many of us who are people-pleasers fear the disapproval of man more than the disapproval of God. "Fear of man will prove to be a snare, but whoever trusts in the Lord is kept safe" (Proverbs 29:25 NIV).

We fail to be a *watchman on the wall* when we shirk our responsibility of not warning others about ungodly attitudes and actions. "But if the watchman sees war coming and doesn't blow the trumpet, warning the people . . . I'll hold the watchman responsible for the bloodshed of any unwarned sinner" (Ezekiel 33:6 MSG).

Wisdom is vital if we are to speak the truth in love when we confront someone. When we fail to speak into another's life, we become an enabler, allowing them to continue doing and/or saying unacceptable things. As a result, they usually remain unchanged. That stifles their spiritual growth and sets a bad example for others.

When we become aware of a problem that needs to be addressed, it's a signal to pray for the right timing and the wisdom to know when and what to say. I frequently pray the Holy Spirit will give me the words I'm to say if I'm to speak to someone about his behavior.

Clearing Past Records

Joe was a major league football player as well as a new Christian. Going over his past, he remembered a time in high school when he'd taken advantage of a girl. He prayed that if God wanted him to contact her and ask her forgiveness, He'd give him that opportunity.

A couple of weeks later, this high school friend telephoned Joe. She told him she was passing through town and would like to congratulate him on making it into a major league.

Since they hadn't seen each other in years, Joe knew God had arranged the appointment. His throat was dry. He hesitated a moment and asked, "Can I meet you for a short visit at a local restaurant?" She agreed, but said she could only stay thirty minutes. On the way to the restaurant, Joe's anxiety rose because he didn't know how she'd respond to this long overdue apology.

When they met, they hugged in a rather stiff and meaningless way. After ordering a cup of coffee and a few minutes of superficial conversation, Joe put his cup down. "Diane, I prayed and asked God for an opportunity to meet with you to ask your forgiveness for the way I violated you in high school."

Diane bit here lip and tears began to fill her eyes. She cried softly. "I've tried to get over that, but I've held bitterness toward you over the years. So I need to ask your forgiveness for the anger I harbored over what happened."

Each acknowledged their forgiveness. In parting, they embraced in warm reconciliation. They expressed a desire to pick up their friendship under far different circumstances.

If we ask, God usually opens a door for us to deal with situations that need closure. I've even asked God to let someone who died years ago know I've forgiven them for ways they hurt me.

The Basis for all Relationships

Our ultimate relationship of course, is with God. As His child, it is imperative to both talk and listen to Him. We communicate with Him through prayer, journaling and one-on-one conversations with the Creator of the Universe and invite His wisdom to flow through our daily experiences.

Insight and wisdom seldom come when we're preoccupied with the rush of everyday activities. It is essential to deliberately pull aside for specific times to be alone with the Father. Some find the only place on the job to escape is to retreat to the bathroom.

The mother of John Wesley had eighteen children. The only way she found to be alone with God was to sit in her rocking chair and cover her head with her apron—a signal to her family that she was in prayer and should not to be disturbed. This bit of quiet time under her apron gave her the strength to deal with the pressures involved with such a large family.

Lord, help me set aside more "apron-time." Teach me to be an example others will follow.

SCRIPTURES TO CONSIDER

Proverbs 29:25
Ezekiel 33:6
1 Corinthians 4:18-20
Ephesians 4:29

QUESTIONS FOR DISCUSSION

1. Have you had a problem in a relationship because you were misunderstood? Explain.

2. Do you feel you are able to express yourself well in most situations? Are there exceptions?

3. What type of people are difficult for you to communicate with?

4. When you are emotionally upset, how does this affect your ability to listen?

5. Have you ever allowed you opinions or prejudices to keep you from understanding another person's point of view?

6. How do you communicate feelings with body language?

26

LISTEN TO MY HEART

I don't listen well when I'm anxious to talk

When we hear the word communication, we may think of conversations that are casual and superficial chit-chat. However, effective listening is every bit as important as talking, if not more so. It is easier to teach a person how to speak than it is to teach them to become a good listener.

A friend was very knowledgeable, yet when he and his wife were in a group, he seldom entered into the discussion. His wife asked why he didn't give his input, since he had so much to offer. He shrugged, "When I'm talking, I don't learn anything new. When I listen, I have an opportunity to learn more."

Many of us are self-absorbed and anxious to impress those around us with how much we know. It's pathetic when we pretend we're an authority when we know very little about the subject people are talking about.

There's a tendency not to listen when people are speaking, because we're darting ahead, thinking about the two cents worth we want to contribute to the conversation. An insightful proverb tells us. "it's better to be thought a fool and remain silent than to speak and remove all doubt."

The Big Ear

In the room where my husband did his counselor training, there was huge picture of an ear on the wall behind the counselee. It was a reminder for the counselor-trainee to listen carefully to what their clients were saying. Since God gave us two ears and one mouth, He may well have intended for us to listen twice as much as we talk.

Once I had a condition similar to "swimmer's ear" which made it difficult for me to hear well. My doctor found I had hardened wax blocking my eardrum that needed to be removed. An even worse affliction is a hardened opinion which also blocks our ability to hear what others are saying.

Listening to God and Others

Listening is a way to show keen interest—when we hang on every word. I have a daughter-in-law that listens carefully to what I say. I can simply express a slight interest in a piece of jewelry, a pretty vase or some other object, and long after I've forgotten about it, she'll give it to me wrapped as a gift for my birthday or Christmas. She listens attentively in order to show love in a meaningful way.

We're awarded the blessing of being able to listen to what God says. In the context of everyday living, His wisdom is revealed through hidden messages in His Word, other's comments or situations. When I fail to listen to God, it makes me wonder how anxious He is to listen to me.

The power of Jesus' life no doubt came from His continuous and intimate communication with the Father. His conduit for listening was large and remained open for the direction and strength He needed.

"Don't fool yourself into thinking that you are a listener when you are anything but, letting the Word go in one ear and out the other. Act on what you hear! Those who hear and don't act are like those who glance in the mirror, walk away, and two minutes later have no idea who they are, what they look like" (James 1:22 MSG).

There are times when I am jabbering away and someone stops me with, "What did you just say?" Because of the lack of meaningful communication, I may stare with a blank expression, "I don't know. I wasn't listening either." Possibly my husband was right when he said, "My wife, generally speaking, is generally speaking."

God Listens

Though God knows our needs, He still expects us to express our desires to Him, along with being thankful for what He's already done. It is astonishing to know we can ask anything in line with the Holy Spirit's wisdom and God is not only willing, but anxious to grant our request. It makes me wonder why I don't spend more time asking, knocking and seeking what He wants for my life and then to pray with the assurance that my prayers *will* be answered.

God *listens*. Someone expressed it well. "If we knit in the ends of each day with prayer; it's not likely to come unraveled in the middle."

One evening my kitchen sink stopped up. I laid on my back under the sink and unscrewed one pipe, but with every ounce of strength I could muster, I couldn't loosen the other. I was tired and my hands were sore from the strain of trying to force it to open.

The phone rang. It was a friend who asked how I was doing. When I explained my frustration, she said, "Let's pray about it." She prayed, "Lord, give her strong hands to unscrew the pipe."

After she hung up, I called my next door neighbor to see if she had a pipe wrench I could borrow. She suggested I come over and we'd look though her tool box. As I walked up her sidewalk, I found her standing outside talking to her yard man. He'd come to tell her it was too late to mow her yard, but he'd be back the following morning. As he turned to go to his truck, I called to him, "Do you have a minute to help me?" He nodded and replied, "Sure," and followed me inside. He was able to unscrew the pipe. I cleaned out the goop, and he put it back together. As he left, I handed him a little money. I was shocked to tears when it dawned on me how carefully God had listened and answered my friend's prayer, "Give her strong hands."

God does listen, down to the nth degree. He's aware of what we do and every blink of the eye. He watches how we spend our time, listens to what we say.

And with His stethoscope of wisdom, He checks the heartbeat of our soul.

Divine Aid

The Holy Spirit prays with and for us. He is our divine interpreter. The Holy Spirit understands God's will for us and takes our simple prayers and reconstructs them until they are in harmony with the Father's plan.

"If we don't know how or what to pray, it doesn't matter. He does our praying in and for us, making prayer out of our wordless sighs, our aching groans. He knows us far better than we know ourselves, knows our pregnant condition, and keeps us present before God. That's why we can be so sure that every detail in our lives of love for God is worked into something good" (Romans 8:26-28 MSG).

Earn the Right to Speak

In some of our sessions at our retreat at Hidden Manna, we use an activity in which the group sits in a circle for a discussion. The rule is that no one has permission to speak until he can accurately summarize what the previous speaker has said. It is necessary for a person to listen in order to add appropriate comments.

Following this exercise, we challenge the group to list reasons why they stop listening to another person. The following are some of their responses:

- I'm thinking about what I'm going to say next.
- I disagree with what the speaker is saying.
- I'm bored.
- I'm distracted because I'm thinking about something else.
- I don't understand what the person is talking about.
- I'm anxious to be on my way.

Critical Words

A person with a critical spirit will often cause those around them to discount what they have to say. Such a person seems to be on a witch hunt to find something—anything to judge and condemn. They ridicule, belittle and shame others behind their backs as well as to their face. Their putdowns have as much potential danger as a smoldering campfire left unattended. "It only takes a spark, remember, to set off a forest fire. A careless, wrongly placed word can do that. By our speech we can ruin the world, turn harmony into chaos, throw mud on a reputation, send the whole world up in smoke. . ." (James 3:5 MSG).

The faintest overdose of criticism is capable of destroying one's self-image and self-confidence. "Don't pick on people, jump on their failures, criticize their faults—unless, of course, you want the same treatment" (Matthew 7:1-2 MSG).

The Dilemma

There's a conflict between wanting to reveal ourselves and a tendency to conceal who we really are. We'd like to be transparent, but that is counterbalanced by a fear that by speaking up, we'll make ourselves vulnerable for rejection. *What if we're betrayed with what we've shared?* Secrets can open a can of worms for judgment to wiggle out. Knowing this, it is wise to pick our confidants carefully.

Carried to the extreme, we hide our true selves behind masks and facades. We bump shells and play a form of hide and seek, hoping others won't find the "real me."

The masterful art of communication and friendship is for us to listen without pre-judging, condemning or criticizing what others believe or have done. Wisdom encourages us to express our input in an articulate and succinct way—then drop it. Jesus left us a perfect example when He spoke to Judas the night he betrayed him. "What you must do, do" said Jesus. "Do it and get it over with" (John 13:27 MSG). He didn't preach to him or condemn him, yet there's no doubt Judas knew where Jesus stood.

Be There

In the depth of a person's sadness or grief, our mere presence may be the most powerful message we can send. Words may get in the way of the message. By being there for others, we let them know how much we care. When we are touched to the point of weeping with them, pride slithers out the door. It has been said that when a person leaks from his eyes, his head isn't likely to swell.

Our goal should be to express genuine empathy as we perceive how circumstances feel to another person—to know how to capture their frame of reference, to understand what it's like to be in their situation. "My dear friends, what I'd like you to do is to try to put yourselves in my shoes . . . . You were sensitive and kind then . . ." (Galatians 4:12 MSG).

However, we get into trouble when we assume we know all about what someone is going through. I bite my tongue and try to keep from being irritated when someone tells me, "I know *exactly* how you feel." Even if they've been through similar circumstances, no one can totally relate to someone else. There are too many factors involved to perfectly line up with another's pain. Simply telling another person we're sorry they're hurting is usually sufficient. If appropriate, we may add, "I can relate somewhat, because I've been through a similar experience."

I had to chuckle when visiting a patient in a mental hospital as she sobbed, "My husband died. He was just sitting there eating and fell over dead."

I tried to comfort her. "I'm sorry. I also lost my husband."

She wailed louder, "But my husband is not coming back." Oh, well.

It is also in poor taste when someone is experiencing great pain and an acquaintance plays one-upmanship. In their insensitivity, they insert a story of their own, presenting something worse than their "friends" problem. It tends to invalidate the pain the grieving person is facing. This rude intrusion focuses on another problem and offers little comfort to the one with a recent loss.

Act Like You Care

One of the reasons people have a pet is that they feel free to talk to an animal about anything. Our youngest son, Chip, had a dog that was his closest companion. When he was having a bad day, he'd say, "Toto is the only one that understands me."

When a person talks to an animal, it goes no further. Often this furry friend comes close and appears to be compassionate and caring. People would do well to practice similar techniques. Animals are used in therapy, especially dogs, not only with children, but also with great success in retirement homes and hospitals.

Someone asked me, "Don't you get lonesome? You don't even have a pet." I smiled. "Oh, I have a number of pet peeves to keep me company, and I'm not such bad company for myself." (Need I tell them I'm never alone?)

Examples of affirming touch:

It has been suggested that the average person needs at least four hugs a day. My husband, a psychologist, suggested people not forget to hug the widows, since they have fewer opportunities to meet their quota.

Often touch has the potential of expressing concern better than words. Briefly placing your hand on the forearm or shoulder transfers meaningful concern for another. One of the most effective messages in times of stress, grief, or happy occasions is an arm around another's shoulder or a brief embrace.

A tender touch can be a jewel more precious than a string of well polished words—as carefully selected as a string of pearls.

- At the church I attend, many welcome one another with a hug.
- Early Christians showed affection for one another when they followed the admonition, "Holy embraces all around. All the churches of Christ send their warmest greetings" (Romans 16:16 MSG).
- Jesus responded to a prostitute who expressed genuine love for Him through touch. "She has rained tears on my feet and dried them with her hair. You gave me no greeting, but from the time I arrived she hasn't quit kissing my feet. . ." (Luke 7:45 MSG).

Lord, teach me how to convey that I care—through my words, my body language and my touch. May my prayers to you not be limited to asking for things while failing to praise You for all You've done. Help me listen carefully for Your guidance to successfully walk out the sequence of events You place before me today.

SCRIPTURES TO CONSIDER

James 3:5–6
Matthew 7:1–3
John 13:27
Galatians 4:14
Proverbs 29:25
Ezekiel 33:6

QUESTIONS FOR DISCUSSION

1. What causes you to stop listening to a speaker?

2. Do you listen to others in a group, or do you do most of the talking?

3. Can you think of times when you were either hurt or hurt someone else because of misunderstandings?

4. How does it make you feel when you realize people aren't listening to you? Explain.

5. Do you at least make an attempt to understand those who have a different opinion from yours?

SECTION VIII
HARVEST TIME

27

THE WORLD NEEDS LOVE

Let your life be a sermon

Love didn't break through the clouds for the first time with the coming of the Son, but Jesus challenged His disciples to reach out with a new dimension of love that was strong enough to grip the heart of the world. He told His disciples He must go away, but God would send His Holy Spirit to be with them.

God didn't simply send directions, but a part of Himself as the Guide for us to follow.

Those "born of water and the Spirit" were to receive a portion of His divinity to empower them to follow His example. Incredible! God offered Himself, His Son and His Spirit—all three parts of the Godhead—to become the secret ingredients to give us the ability to walk out His legacy of love.

It is possible to give without love, but it is *impossible* to love without giving.

In first John, chapter 4, he mentions some form of the word "love" twenty-eight times. John challenges us: "He who does not love has not become acquainted with God—does not and never did know Him; for God is love . . . if we love one another, God abides (lives and remains) in us and His love . . . is perfected—in us" (1 John 4:8, 12 AMP). In essence, John warns that if we don't live a life reflecting love, we've missed the boat as well as eternal life.

Not a Natural Lover

The Apostle Paul hunted down Christians and persecuted them. But when he encountered Jesus, his life was transformed. He penned the "psalm of love" in first Corinthians 13, setting up beautiful, but challenging standards. Paul emphasizes that we can speak in tongues of men and angels, have the gift of prophesy, understand all mysteries, have enough faith to move mountains or be burned at the stake, but it counts for nothing if we've not gotten a handle on love. A life without love is a flat zero. On a scale of one to ten, it doesn't even register. *Lord, help our lives to count for something of value by filling us with the kind of love Jesus modeled.*

Christian Examples of Love

A preacher of a huge church got up one Sunday morning and walked to the pulpit and spoke three words: "Love one another," and turned and sat down. Several in the congregation grimaced and looked at one another. The preacher came to the pulpit two more times to repeat this charge and again returned to his seat. People squirmed in their pews.

Finally, one of the members got up and walked to another section in the assembly and handed a struggling fellow Christian a roll of money. A few minutes later, another rose and went to a person with whom he'd had a conflict and asked for forgiveness and hugged him. People began to weep as they reached out in love to other members of their congregation. Families wept as they acknowledged how much they truly loved one another.

The minister said it was undoubtedly the most powerful message he'd ever delivered. He saw love in action with enough supernatural power to transform lives. "Now that you have purified yourselves by obeying the truth so that you have sincere love for your brothers, love one another deeply, with all your hearts . . ." (1 Peter 1:22 NIV).

An early Christian writer, Jerome, tells us that when the Apostle John grew old, he was carried to the assembly of the saints. When asked to speak, he would repeat, "Little children, love one another. Little children, love one another." As his weak voice trailed off, some became impatient and asked John why he kept saying the same thing over and over. According to history, his simple explanation was, "Because it is the Lord's command, and if it is fulfilled, it is enough."

Tertullian, who lived in the second century, recorded the impressions Christians made on the world: "See how they love one another. They are ready to die for each other." *Lord, forgive us when we won't make an effort to walk across the street for a brother or sister in Christ.*

In the fourth century, Chrysostom penned, "Miracles do not so much attract the heathen as their mode of life and nothing so much as a life of love. The heathen admire our doctrines, but they are hindered by our way of life." The love that had characterized the early church had waned and was losing its power to impact the unbeliever as it had previously.

A Legacy to Follow

The Apostle Peter had the reputation of being impulsive and impatient, but his writings are saturated with loving kindness. All Jesus' apostles were earthy men like us, with different personalities, but all were transformed when they walked alongside the Epitome of Love. It's reassuring to know God is searching for those who will pick up the baton of love, to continue to run the race set before them.

Christians are to be "Living Stones" held together with the mortar of love. Just as a small child can push over a stack of bricks without mortar, a child of the devil can wreak havoc in a church or a family lacking tender loving care. But it's quite a different matter when Living Stones are bound together by love. Satan and all the demons of hell can't tear them apart.

Golden Thread

Just as a golden thread woven into cloth enhances the beauty and value of a piece of fabric, so love is the "golden thread" laced throughout the warp and weft of godly lives. All other graces and virtues are to be intertwined with love. Could this golden thread possibly be the material out of which robes of righteousness are made?

The parents of six-year old Bobby★ asked him if he would be willing to give a bone marrow transplant to his three-year-old little sister, in an effort to save her life from the death-threatening disease of leukemia. He didn't answer immediately, but that night as his mother tucked him in bed to say his prayers, he looked up and said, "Mom, I've decided I want to have that operation to help save Cindy's★ life."

Several days later they were at the hospital for the procedure, and the medical team was ready to roll Bobby into the operating room. His parents tearfully kissed him, thanking and telling him how proud they were of him. They held his hands and prayed. He looked up with a bit of fear in his eyes and asked, "When will I begin to die?" His love was demonstrated in a commitment that he believed would require him to give his life. This is the deepest kind of love. "Greater love has no man than this: to lay down one's life for one's friends" (John 15:13 NIV).

My daughter-in-law offered to give a kidney to a friend who was on dialysis and in desperate need of a new kidney. She made this offer so this friend might live. This is also an example of an incredible act of love.

Love should be the hallmark of the Christian life. The story of the members of the early Jerusalem church selling their possessions to share everything is so touching. It was not required or demanded, but a beautiful expression of spontaneous love for needy brothers and sisters in Christ.

Do we dare follow this challenging example?

Loving in Large and Small Ways

No doubt Christianity would explode in the world today if we took the opportunity to show love in each interaction. If this kind of love was birthed in the home, it would swell and flow out the door as one of the most powerful sermons ever delivered. We'd be forced to jump out of the way of Christianity spreading and flowing throughout the community.

God would have Christians as lighthouses of love for those who are adrift in icy seas of loneliness.

Love, as the Fruit of the Spirit, is most evident when we serve others. It is amazing to me that the Bible teaches that the more lowly our service to others, the greater He esteems us. "Then he said to them, ". . . For it is the one who is least among you all who is the greatest" (Luke 9:48 NIV).

A man at church married a woman who has muscular dystrophy. Though she stays upbeat and active and has developed some incredible ways of being productive, she's incapable of doing anything physical for herself. Her husband feeds her and cares for her every need. It is a 24/7 challenge. She blows into a mouthpiece to move her wheelchair from place to place. Curious, I asked, "Jack, how were you able to commit to marry her, knowing she'd be totally dependent on you for the rest of her life?" He shrugged his shoulders slightly, "I suppose it's what you'd call love."

To experience the love of God is like being initiated into a secret rite that defies human explanation.

Love Is Tested in Terrible Circumstances

A Christian friend of mine was imprisoned four times in an ungodly country and treated without mercy because of her Christian faith. In one prison, she was in such a tiny cell, she had no choice but to stand, sit or kneel.

One day the guards told her she would die the following day, but they'd come to grant her one final request. She asked, "Would you allow me to sing?" They glanced at one another with a questioned look, but nodded their permission. She sang a couple of Christian hymns over and over. One of those hymns was *Amazing Grace*.

After singing for a period of time, she looked out through the bars and tears were streaming down the faces of her guards. They could not comprehend this kind of unwavering faith and love of God. The Father's love flowed out through prison bars and touched the hearts of those cruel guards.

For an unknown reason, this godly sister was released. She continued to cling tenaciously to her deep commitment to God. She said her only regret was that she had not memorized more scripture before being imprisoned.

Equipped to Give

God spurred Jesus on by expressing His deep love for Him. It must have created even a deeper bond between the Father and

Jesus when Almighty God told Him, "You are my Son, chosen and marked by my love, pride of my life" (Luke 3:22 MSG).

When a person grows up in a family where love is expressed in the home through words as well as actions, the children will very likely learn to speak the language of love. Since love is a universal language, no doubt it will be the language spoken in heaven throughout eternity—with or without words. It's time for God's children to become fluent in speaking the language well.

Lord, give me the grace to speak love similar to the way You shower Your unconditional love on those of us who call you Father. Even when people rile against You, persecute You and yell at You with degrading curses, You reach out to them with forgiveness and compassion.

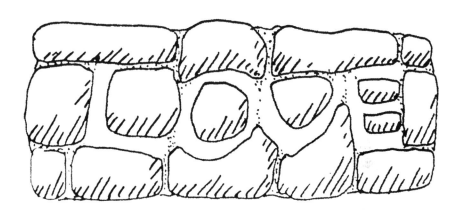

SCRIPTURES TO CONSIDER

1 John 4:8
1 Peter 1:22
Matthew 23:11-12
1 Corinthians 13 (Read the entire chapter)

QUESTIONS FOR DISCUSSION

1. How can you love someone that rubs you the wrong way?

2. Would those who know you best say you were a loving person? Explain.

3. What do others do that make you feel loved?

4. Explain how someone has shown you a great act of love. (Besides God, the Holy Spirit or Jesus.)

5. How might Christians show more love to members as well as non-members.

6. In what ways should a Christian's love differ from those who are not Christians?

28

ABIDING JOY
Our source of strength

A twinkle in the eye is evidence of joy rising from the heart. Joy helps us to skip through the mud puddles of life—those dirty dips along the road. It's the anti-depressant prescribed by the Great Physician.

Joy creates air currents that lift us from valleys of despair.

Genuine Joy

Joy saturates our cells. But like a muscle—if not strengthened, our exuberance grows weak and ineffective. The muscles that curl our lips give way, and the edges of our mouths droop. Paul urges us to make joy an essential part of the Christian life, "Rejoice in the Lord always. I will say it again: Rejoice!" (Philippians 4:4 NIV). His repeated charge emphasizes the importance of this admonition.

It doesn't seem logical that rejoicing should be a commandment. But it does imply that joy is a choice. We're to cultivate it like any healthy behavior until it becomes a habit.

When God ignites a spark in our heart and blows a kiss on it, joy bursts into flame.

Paul admonishes us: "Rejoice in the Lord always." Joy is more than a spontaneous response that's directly related to something good happening at the moment.. David tells us, "Weeping may stay for the night, but rejoicing comes in the morning" (Psalms 30:5 NIV).

Joy is a jewel we wear, regardless of the occasion.

True Joy

Years ago, I prayed to be filled with the Holy Spirit. I laughed for three days. Not a flippant sort of laughter, but overflowing glee, expressing sheer joy and praise, birthed from the Holy Spirit's blessing. It was not the kind of joy that's dependent on "happenstance" but an abiding trust in knowing that God uses every circumstance to prepare good things for His children.

Genuine joy isn't from the teeth out, with a pasty smile, but a lilting freedom that flows from deep within a heart. It glows and lights up the lives of others. Joy proclaims victory in every situation.

It's natural and easy for us to be full of joy when things go *our* way or work according to *our* plans or desires. But unlike the world, joy is a secret ingredient concealed within the worst of circumstances. God gives a Christian something to laugh about that pulls us through dark days. "Day and night I'll stick with God; I've got a good thing going and I'm not letting go. I'm happy from the inside out, and from the outside in, I'm firmly formed . . . Now you've got my feet on the life path, all radiant from the shining of your face. Ever since you took my hand, I'm on the right way" (Psalms 16:8-11 MSG). I pray those who don't know Christ will experience this blessing.

Health Benefits of Joy

Research has proven joy greatly enhances our immune system, and it definitely creates a healthy environment for those around us. "A cheerful heart is good medicine, but a broken spirit saps a person's strength" (Proverbs 17:22 NLT).

Joy is the medication prescribed and laughter is the poultice that draws the sting from the wounds of disappointment. "Deceit is in the hearts of those who plot evil, but those who promote peace have joy" (Proverbs 12:20 NIV).

In Solomon's description of what we call *a worthy woman* in Proverbs 31, he explains, "she can laugh at the days to come." This woman latched on to the blessed assurance that God holds the keys to the future in His hands. God is on His throne and all is right with the world. I too can laugh at times to come. This sunshine in my life warms my soul, causing my faith to grow.

- Joy is the chlorophyll that keeps us green, full of life and growing.

- It warms our hearts and bubbles up with blossoms of laughter.
- Joy is a delightful spirit that sparkles, shines and sings.
- Joy is like a bird we release to fly in the open heavens—its musical song filling the air.
- Joy is a magnet that draws people.

Joy in the lives of God's children is like a good Pied Piper enticing the world with a melodic call to follow Jesus. "Laugh and the world laughs with you." Smiles increase our face value, and joy is contagious. "In all my prayers for all of you, I always pray with joy because of your partnership in the gospel from the first day until now, being confident of this, that he who began a good work in you will carry it on to completion until the day of Christ Jesus" (Philippians 1:4-7 NIV).

In college, I dated a young man that had an unusual but lilting laughter. He felt the same way about my laugh. When something tickled our funny bones, we went from chuckles to deep belly laughter as we nearly fell out of our chairs in sheer joy, pointing fingers at one another.

Tests of Joy
- When we cannot rejoice over what's happening in our life, we can simply smile because we know God's grace and mercy is wrapped around every circumstance.
- When we're lonely, we can rejoice that He is with us. "Be happy (in your faith) and rejoice and be glad-hearted continually. . ." (1 Thess. 5:16 AMP).
- If you have a flat tire when it's raining and you're in a hurry, rejoice. God hasn't abandoned you. Accept this as a prime time for patience to grow.
- Suppose your plans don't work out as you thought they should. God may have better plans in store for you.
- What if you lose your job or suffer financial difficulties? Understand that your faith is tested in difficult times. Ultimately, God is your provider.
- What about the times when you're rejected or mistreated by

others? You can depend on God to always be there with His unconditional love.

- What are you to do when you or a family member encounters some misfortune? You can continue to remain spiritually healthy. "Thank (God) in everything—no matter what the circumstances may be, be thankful and give thanks; for this is the will of God for you (who are) in Christ Jesus (the Revealer and Mediator of that will)" (1 Thessalonians 5:18 AMP).

- If there is nothing else we can rejoice about, we choose to rejoice that God is all-knowing and all-powerful. He can bring victory out of every situation that rears its ugly head.

Joy in Difficulties

"My friends, be glad, even if you have a lot of trouble. You know that you learn to endure by having your faith tested. But you must learn to endure everything, so that you will be completely mature and not lacking in anything" (James 1:2-4 CEV).

In difficult times, I remind myself that God is still in control. Long before I was born, He held the answer to every problem I would ever face. Therefore, today I choose to carry joy in my small black bag—one like a doctor carries. It contains my little black book, called the Bible, which offers a healing solution for every sickening attack.

The beauty of our lives shines brightest when others observe how we handle difficult situations. "Pure gold put in the fire comes out of it proved pure; genuine faith put through this suffering comes out proved genuine . . ." You never saw him, yet you love him. You still don't see him, yet you trust him—with laughter and singing." (1 Peter 1:6-6 MSG).

Joy is the oil of gladness that soothes and softens the personality of man. It can't be crafted from a formula. God gave us laughter. And a song in our heart causes the sunshine in our souls to glow. Joy is the silver lining that surrounds every dark cloud, assuring us that the Son is over and above everything—ready at any moment to burst forth in all His glory

Any one of us can be upbeat and happy-go-lucky when there's money in the bank, when our health is good, and we're surrounded by those who love and care for us. But things are not always "rosy."

It's sad, but ideal situations have a tendency to slither away or melt in our hands.

The old adage "into each life some rain must fall" may sound trite, but it's true. Not only does life rain on our parade, but at times horrific storms come to beat against our peace and joy. "Dear friends, don't be bewildered or surprised when you go through the fiery trials ahead, for this is not a strange, unusual thing that is going to happen to you. Instead, be really glad—because these trials will make you partners with Christ in His suffering, and afterwards you will have the wonderful joy of sharing His glory in that coming day when it will be displayed" (1 Peter 4:12-13 NIV).

Joy in Practice

In Philippi, Paul expressed supreme joy in the face of the most trying difficulties. He and Silas were arrested and beaten, then placed in stocks in a dark, damp and dirty dungeon. It was no Holiday or Hilton Inn. But God had a purpose. And these committed followers knew the Father well enough to cling to Him. They continued to pray, sing and praise God in that stinky, horrible prison.

Paul and Silas were not bitter because of their pain and discomfort, nor did they feel God has forsaken them. They rejoiced and radiated peace in their darkest hour. It thrills me to read of the great miracle God performed in those circumstances. He expressed His pleasure by opening the prison doors to release them. It makes me wonder if prison doors in my own life are locked because of the lack of joy I've exhibited in dealing with problems.

The letter Paul wrote to the church at Philippi at this very same place was incredibly joyous in its tone and wording. The reference to joy is used more than fifteen times in this short epistle. I can't imagine how he stayed so upbeat when trapped under his circumstances. (Obviously, he was not "under" the circumstances, but standing tall above them.)

Joy of the Holy Spirit

Joy is often identified with being filled with the Spirit. Reference is made to being anointed with joy. When the Holy Spirit filled me with joy, almost immediately, the enemy came against me in an attempt to steal this precious gift. It took concerted effort to hold fast to this anointing of joy.

"God's kingdom isn't about eating and drinking. It is about pleasing God, about living in peace, and about true happiness. All this comes from the Holy Spirit. If you serve Christ in this way, you will please God and be respected by people" (Romans 14:17-18 CEV).

Joy in Jesus

Jesus' birth was announced as the angels sang, *Joy To the World.* "The shepherds left their flocks... and the star they had seen in the east went ahead of them until it stopped over the place where the child was. When they saw the star, they were overjoyed" (Matthew 2:10 NIV). "But the angel said to them, 'Do not be afraid. I bring you good news of great joy that will be for all people. Today in the town of David a Savior has been born to you; He is Christ the Lord" (Luke 2:10-11 NIV).

Jesus experienced joy during his life. The same source of joy He had is available to us. "At that time Jesus, full of joy through the Holy Spirit, said, 'I praise you, Father, Lord of heaven and earth, because you have hidden these things from the wise and learned, and revealed them to little children. Yes, Father, for this was your good pleasure'" (Luke 10:21 NIV). Since joy was such a vital part of our Savior's life, it emphasizes that His joy should be an integral part of our lives.

Even in dying, Jesus expressed joy. "Fixing our eyes on Jesus . . . For the joy set before Him, He endured the cross, scorning its shame, and sat down at the right hand of the throne of God" (Hebrews 12:2 NIV). We too must learn how to look beyond our trials to the reward God has reserved for those who endure.

The glimpse we have of heaven is a picture full of love, peace, joy and thanksgiving. "To him who is able to keep you from stumbling and to present you before his glorious presence without fault and with great joy—" (Jude 24 NIV). Shouts of joy are as springs gushing from deep wells of love.

Joy Is Expressed in Praise

In current language, joy is the "pep pill' for the Christian. ". . .for the joy of the Lord is your strength" (Nehemiah 8:10 NIV). Joy neutralizes negative, pessimistic and critical attitudes. All these assaults come from the devil himself. He uses all these tactics to weaken us in his attempt to utterly destroy us. Thank you, Lord. We celebrate the victory because of the strength that comes from Your joy.

Joy
Sweetens the disposition,
Enhances the personality,
Strengthens our faith and
Encourages our spirits.
It lightens our loads,
Deepens our love,
Inspires our friends, and
Gives evidence of the Holy Spirit.
It makes us like Jesus,
Prepares us for heaven, and
Pleases God our Father!
LLL

The Christian isn't promised he will always have smooth sailing in life, but God's Word teaches us we can have joy in the journey.

Lord, may others find us joyful. And it won't be because we're unaware of the seriousness of our situation. It's because we continue to look beyond the challenges facing us. We've read the end of the book You wrote. We believe it and are prepared to stand alongside You in the winner's circle.

SCRIPTURES TO CONSIDER

Philippians 4:4-7
Proverbs 17:22
Proverbs 15:13
Psalms 30:5
1 Thessalonians 5:28
1 Peter 4:12-13
Romans 14:17-18
Hebrews 12:2
Jude 24
Nehemiah 8:10

QUESTIONS FOR DISCUSSION

1. Tell of several ways you experience joy.

2. How can you be joyful, even when things seem to be going wrong?

3. Can we look past the trouble we are currently going through by knowing if we know God will ultimately work everything out for good in the end? Explain.

4. Do you consider yourself to be a happy person?

5. What are things you can focus on that will give you more joy?

6. How does your thoughts-life influence your joy?

29

THE INHERITANCE
JESUS LEFT

The world's best tranquilizer

"Peace, peace, sweet peace, wonderful gift of God's love." The message in this old hymn is like the sun breaking through the clouds near the end of an overcast and dreary day. The world seeks peace at the conference table, between nations and within families. But most of all, we yearn for peace within our own soul. Come with me, the search is on!

Last Words

When my husband, Carey, was dying, he asked me to resign my teaching job at the prison. He said, "I've never felt comfortable about you being there." I liked my job and wouldn't have quit if he'd not made this request. But I felt it was right and good to honor his last wish.

The last words people speak have an impact on our lives. The last words I heard my dad say before he died were, "Sweetheart, there's someone at the door, let him in." I wondered if he saw angels coming to take him home.

Jesus' last words before His death were some of His most profound: "Peace I leave with you; my peace I give you. I do not give to you as the world gives. Do not let your hearts be troubled and do not be afraid" (John 14:27 NIV). Since trouble and fear are the arch enemies of peace, Jesus spoke to the source of our problems—the world that comes against us.

Jesus' farewell message left a treasured legacy of hope. The men who clung to Jesus had forsaken their former life to walk alongside the One that would overcome the world. Some walked away from fishing nets and left them lying on the seashore so they could become fishers of men. They followed with a staunch confidence that Jesus possessed the secrets of abundant living. Their inheritance of peace was given for them to "pay forward." This was to be passed down to every generation until He returns as the Prince of Peace.

For some three years, these men followed their Savior. Just as the Son of man had no place to lay His head, they gave up worldly comforts and pleasures. Not only that, but they also braced themselves to face persecution He'd told them would come against them. But Jesus promised that peace would undergird every circumstance. Serenity could reign over every challenge thrown at them—even death. Stephen confirmed this as he was being stoned to death as he cried out, "Lord Jesus, receive my spirit."

The Source of Jesus' Peace

Jesus left them (and us) with what many would consider to be a strange inheritance—peace. Stranger still, we can "take it to the bank." He modeled peace by remaining serene as He was led to be crucified.

The end was forecast, "He was led like a sheep to the slaughter, and as a lamb before its sheerer is silent, so He did not open his mouth" (Acts 8:32 NIV). This incomprehensible peace came about because He committed to *stay* in the eye of the storm—in the center of His Father's will.

Jesus reminded his disciples, "I give you peace, the kind of peace that only I can give. It isn't like the peace that this world can give. So don't be worried or afraid" (John 14:27 CEV).

Peace was bequeathed as our greatest safe-guard, our shield to hold up against the onslaught of the world and all its assaults. *Thank you, Lord, this promise has remained valid down through generations and given to every one of us.*

The Search for "Out of this World" Peace

The world thinks peace is obtained by doing what you want, when you want it, and satisfying every whim because we have the resources to buy anything our hearts desire. In a sense, the criterion for worldly peace is based on selfishness. "Take care! Protect yourself against the least bit of greed. Life is not defined by what you have, even when you have a lot" (Luke 12:15 MSG).

The apostle's new commitment offered no financial support to take care of their physical needs. But their faith caused them to trust that the Lord would provide for all essentials. I believe they realized that most everything the world considers an ingredient for peace failed to be a part of their "deal."

Contrast

Notice the sharp contrast between how the world seeks peace and how we obtain it through Jesus:

THE WORLD	JESUS
Peace comes by not having to work;	Peace comes by serving others;
Peace is obtained by looking out for self;	Peace looks out for others first;
Peace is set on getting the most . . .	Peace resolves to give the most . . .

We'll have the same peace Jesus had if we follow the divine recipe God measured out for us.

"Don't fret or worry. Instead of worrying, pray. Let petitions and praise shape your worries into prayers, letting God know your concerns. Before you know it, a sense of God's wholeness, everything coming together for good, will come and settle you down" (Philippians 4:6-7 MSG).

All Encompassing Peace
- Peace doesn't plan a rebuttal in arguments.
- Peace doesn't take up an offense for another.
- Peace doesn't recap "what might have been."
- Peace doesn't wiggle out of sin with excuses, but confesses and repents of all wrong.
- Peace accepts life even when circumstances don't change.
- Peace understands it takes two to fight or argue.
- Peace searches for the good in others as well as for the good that can come from circumstances.

The peace Jesus offers covers all relationships. It makes it possible for us to have peace with God, ourselves and with others. "Do not let your hearts be troubled. You believe in God; believe also in me" (John 14:1 NIV).

Antidote

Psychological germs that destroy peace are in the air, and we're all exposed to them.

The world is seething with angry and disgruntled people. We must determine not to be contaminated by them. "I'm leaving you well and whole. That's my parting gift to you. Peace. I don't leave you as you're used to being left—feeling abandoned, bereft. So don't be upset. Don't be distraught" (John 14:27 MSG).

Peace comforts us. It's as if God holds us in His arms and rocks us. The lullaby He sings removes all doubt that anything in the universe can destroy this relationship. Pass it on!

Lord, when the world crashes down on me in the form of trials, sickness or financial distress, give me the wisdom and strength to know You specialize in bringing the best out of every circumstance. Help me to hold steady from the inside out to exhibit a peace that is greater than anything the world will ever understand.

SCRIPTURES TO CONSIDER

John 14:27
Acts 8:32
Luke 12:15
John 16:22
Philippians 4:6-7

QUESTIONS FOR DISCUSSION

1. Why was Jesus referred to as the Prince of Peace?

2. Contrast the world's definition of peace with a Christian's definition?

3. What is the first thing you do when bad things happen— worry or pray? Explain.

4. Name things you do to have more peace—even when a bad situation doesn't change?

5. Has your world generally been filled with turmoil or peace? Explain.

6. Why should a Christian be able to remain at peace easier than a non-Christian?

30

THE GREAT PHYSICIAN'S PRESCRIPTION FOR PEACE

Surrounded by a bubble of peace

Paul taught, as well as implemented, the blessed insight the Holy Spirit revealed to him. "Don't be anxious about anything, but pray about everything, with prayers and supplications and with thanksgiving, let your requests be made known to God and the peace of God that passes all understanding will guard your minds and hearts in Christ Jesus (Philippians 4:6-7 NIV).

The first portion of this scripture tells us we are to pray about everything. The typical response for the Christian might be, "Yeah, yeah, I know we're supposed to pray." But we're stopped short when he commands to pray "with thanksgiving."

"Now wait a minute Paul, how in the *world* can we be thankful for bad things that happen while living on this old planet earth?"

But in my spirit I hear him say, "Jesus peace is not *of* this *world*." Uh oh—He has my attention. He implies that if I believe God brings good things from bad, I can be confident that even when I encounter the worst of times, I can maintain inexplicable peace as I wait for the best of times.

Steps to Walking in Peace

I cannot and *will* not be shaken by encounters where the devil pounces on me with his devious schemes.

"Back off buster, I've called on Jesus to fight this battle for me."

The Lord's peace erects a barrier to protect my entire being against the enemy's onslaught. When I ask Him, God Almighty stands nearby, and He's willing to offer me protection. His grace is sufficient. How thankful I am for this loving care from our gracious Father that is capable of standing against the world and all the demons of hell.

The last portion of Philippians 4:6-7 reminds us this peace is to guard our minds and hearts. The mind is the intellectual part of man, possessing the ability to think things through, to reason situations out.

It is the place where Satan contrives to drag in confusion, doubt and fear. A peace that guards the mind has the ability to leap over intellectual reasoning, catapulting it into the green pastures of God's peace. By God's grace, I develop the mind of Christ that acts on God's Truth, not my reasoning ability.

The peace that guards my heart holds my emotions intact. I've secured that peace by my commitment to live in such a way that my emotions aren't in charge of my life. Jesus' peace and security are not based on how I feel, but on what I know is the Truth of His Word.

A Deeper Life

When we're fervent in prayer, we're able to shift our concentration from the heat of our struggles to the power that calms the ceaseless stewing of anxiety. Jesus offers the divine solution: "Don't worry about anything: Instead, pray about everything,"

If we aren't careful, worry will consume and suck away our ability to trust God because our faith is weakened. But confident prayer welcomes our King of kings to come against this enemy and rescue us from this terror. His peace is greater than the human mind can understand. It keeps our hearts quiet and at rest, because we are trusting in a Power that is greater than anything this world can devise.

The world's peace is like fool's gold. It sparkles and looks good, but it has no intrinsic value. The world's peace is totally based on circumstances. God's peace is based completely on our trust in Him.

Imagine how a pilot who has been lost in a vast darkness must feel when he suddenly receives a directional beam that guides him to the airport for a safe landing. It is also in blessed relief when we find we've been guided out of the wilderness of doubt and despair.

The Lord's peace is a lighthouse penetrating both darkness and the fog of fear and confusion. It shines from the shore of faith and leads us into a safe harbor.

The Grace of Gratitude

A study found that one of the characteristics of mentally ill people was that they seldom express gratitude. Many of us have been conditioned to take our blessings for granted. No doubt our spirits would be wondrously lifted if we'd begin each day with grateful hearts and vocal expressions of gratitude—not only to God, but also to those surrounding us.

The world has been programmed to focus on bad things. The evening news seldom features good news, but always reports terrible happenings.

In the work-place, we generally hear:

- more gripes than gratitude,
- more complaining than compliments,
- more whining than whistling.

Perhaps it would come as a shock to find the percentage of our prayers that consist of begging and complaining rather than thanking and praising.

Spiritual Tranquilizer

God offers us a spiritual tranquilizer that helps us face all sorts of situations that spring up in our lives. Scripture gives us an everyday illustration. Jesus and the disciples were on their way to Jerusalem when they came to a village where a woman named Martha welcomed them into her home. Martha's sister, Mary, immediately sat at the feet of Jesus to listen to His wisdom. Meanwhile, Martha was fussing over the dinner she was preparing. In her irritation, she came in and asked Jesus if He didn't think it was unfair that Mary didn't help prepare the meal. The subject of priorities arose when Jesus made it clear, she was upset over details, but Mary had chosen something better. *Lord, help us focus on the priorities You have for us.*

When I dropped by a friend's house to leave some papers, she insisted I stay for lunch. I made excuses, but she refused to listen to any of them. Reluctantly, I accepted her invitation. I stepped over clutter and into the kitchen where she removed papers and magazines from a chair so that I could sit down. She smiled, "What do you want, tea or coffee? I know. I'll give you both."

She opened the cabinet and surveyed her supplies briefly before grabbing a jar of peanut butter and a box of crackers. She made no excuses or apologies. When we finished eating that simple fare, she walked me to the door and smiled. "I so enjoyed your visit. I wouldn't have you come by and not eat with me." I thanked her and walked away chuckling. She was comfortable and at peace to offer me the meager resources she had. In doing so, that lady blessed me with genuine hospitality.

Peace or Complacency

The world continues its attacks to destroy the Christian's rights and our peace of mind. A judge is told he must remove the Ten Commandments from the walls of his courtroom or else face a lawsuit.

Others come against officials to force them to take down a manger scene in front of the city hall. Prayer is forbidden in schools and public gatherings. The anti-Christians claim these things are offensive. Our government fails to consider that a vast majority is offended by this threat to undermine our Christian rights. However, in our lack of concern and under the guise of peace, Christians too often remain silent. This isn't an example of peace, but of complacency.

Peace Purifies

The devil promotes ideas that will contaminate our minds, to poison our thinking. But when God's peace and love flow through our thought-life, it washes out the corruption of bad thinking. It makes it possible for the spring-water of God-like thoughts to run fresh and pure again. Living Water splashes over our souls.

Peace is the opposite of anxiety. It's the blessing the world longs for. It is that elusive feeling of calmness, contentment and trust—an extreme blessing to know we're given access. This kind of peace from God is a pillow on which to rest our minds.

"Sis" was the mother hen of our family. Interestingly, her name was Octavene—the oldest of eight. She didn't like her name and insisted we call her *Sis*. When she was diagnosed with stage four cancer that had spread to five major organs, the medical staff gave her from three to six months to live. Friends asked, "Why you?" She shook her head, "Why not me? There's no reason why I should be exempt from trouble."

Through an incredible miracle, she not only recovered, but six months later, her doctor reported he could find no evidence of the disease and assured her no other doctor would be able to tell she'd ever had cancer! He saw no reason to continue chemo-therapy or radiation.

Sis lived another twenty years before she had a heart attack. Within a few months, she moved from an apartment to assisted living, and ultimately to a nursing home. Sis persevered and continued to walk with God, even as she grew old and moved slowly. Her focus remained on the Lord until the end. She'd been in the nursing home about three weeks when one of the aides came by her room one night to see if she'd gotten ready for bed. Sis told her, "I just wish I could go."

"Go where?" the aide questioned.

"I just wish I could go home and be with Jesus."

Less than an hour later, the aide came back to talk to her. Sis had "checked out." Being at peace wherever she was, she'd made her last request. Her gracious Father granted her wish and took her safely home. Sis died at peace with God and man. She was filled with Living Water and splashed it on those surrounding her as she took her dying breath.

Epitaph

I don't want to wait until I die to have, "Rest in Peace" chiseled on my tombstone. If you don't mind, please etch it on my heart now. I want to live my life in such a way that this legacy of peace will be passed on from one generation to the next.

Lord, give us a peace that is not based on circumstances. Rather, give us the Jesus type peace that looks beyond every circumstance, knowing You will see us through and reward us with unimaginable blessings. Wherever I am, whatever happens, give me the grace to say, "It is well with my soul."

SCRIPTURES TO CONSIDER

Philippians 4:6-7
Luke 10:38-42

QUESTIONS FOR DISCUSSION

1. Why is thanksgiving is an important part of peace?

2. Explain why Jesus said His peace was not of this world?

3. Can we still have peace in our hearts, even when we are shaking on the outside?

4. How does a lack of peace affect our countenance?

5. How does a lack of peace in our own lives affect those around us?

6. Does your peace depend on circumstances? Explain.

ABOUT THE AUTHOR

Louise L. Looney is an author and speaker. She has taught all levels of education, including in the prison system and in an underground school in an anti-Christian nation. She directed a Christian retreat center for years. Her book, Hidden Treasures for Golden Years, won the 2011 award for the best book on Christian living. You may contact the author at louisellooney@gmail.com.